LOVE SEEKER

Part One

FOUND

Barbara Ann Quinlan

Copyright © Barbara Ann Quinlan, 2021
Published: 2021 by The Book Reality Experience

ISBN: 978-0-6450629-8-4 Paperback Edition
ISBN: 978-0-6450629-9-1 EBook Edition

This book is a memoir, reflecting the author's present recollections
of experiences over time. This means that some details may vary
from fact. Some names and characteristics have been changed,
some events have been compressed, and some dialogue has been
recreated. Memory can be a fickle thing, so the Author trusts that
any minor errors in times, dates and details of particular events
will be understood.

Some names and identifying details have been changed to protect
the privacy of individuals.

Front Cover Photo: The Author
Cover Design by Luke Buxton | www.lukebuxton.com

To my Teacher
with deep gratitude.

For Laurie

with Love

Author's Note

This book is a memoir and as the dictionary will tell you, a memoir is a historical account or biography written from personal knowledge. This memoir is my memoir and so is written with and from my personal knowledge. Where that differs from the historical record, as decided on, or written, by others, then I can only say, that's not how I recall it.

Where it differs from your own knowledge, should you be in or near to my life, or the situations I describe, then again, I can but say, we see from our own eyes.

Being my present recollections of experiences, tempered by the passing of time, I have no doubt that some details may vary from supposed fact. Some names and characteristics may have been changed, some events compressed, and some dialogue recreated. All I can offer is that despite memory being fickle, I have told no lies, nor included any statements that I believe to be untrue. I offer no hurt, nor malice.

I am and always have been a seeker of Love and so I only offer that within these pages. That you may read them and love them for what they are. A story.

My story.

Barbara
New York City
2021

Chapter One — JM

I see myself walking back up Theophile Gautier in the 16eme district of Paris, just as the evening begins to draw the trees' shadows upon the sidewalk. Ahead, though still in the distance, a man in an elegant overcoat is walking towards me. The light obscures his face, though there is something familiar about his gait. As he continues in his self-assured stride, I sense an awakening within me and quicken my pace directly towards him. "Can it be?" I wonder.

His face is coming into view, and it is clear now that he sees me, too. Strangely, I can feel the apprehension building inside him, the doubt, the disbelief, until finally, there I am, standing directly in his path, face-to-face, eye-to-eye.

"Mais, qu'est-ce que tu veux?" he blurts out before the shock can set in and the awe of love washes over his eyes, widening them. How long ago had he first asked me that question? My answer had given birth to our relationship.

*

I turned 21 in Paris, alone. Now I recall, that was the night we met. I had only just arrived a few days before, after a harrowing night in Amsterdam, where I was forcibly ejected from the only youth hostel I'd ever attempted to stay in. I was never much for curfews. A communal room full of bunk beds was not my style. The hostel manager caught my friend Robyn and me in a bathroom stall where we were trying to smoke hash oil out of a small glass bottle. Suddenly we were thrown down the outside stairs, my 80-pound knapsack tumbling after us as he screamed, "Lesbians!" I wasn't sure if we were being thrown out for breaking curfew, smoking hash oil, or because he thought we were lesbians. Whatever; it was Amsterdam for God's sake!

My first tiny room in Paris was in the servant's quarters on the top floor at 1 Rue Delambre. There was no window. A bare light bulb hung from the ceiling, a showerhead was affixed in the corner, with a plastic curtain to draw around it and a drain on the floor. The bed was a small mattress, also on the floor. Though I had never seen a room like this nor imagined such a lodging, the barren simplicity some-how made me feel stronger. Having quickly realized that I would need to work to stay afloat in Paris, I soon took a job as au pair to a young boy named Fabrice, who lived with his father.

On my birthday, I went down the street to the nearest café and ordered a glass of champagne. I toasted myself and thought how wonderful it was to be alone, where no one knew me and I could perhaps see who I really was out-side the confines of other's concepts. The fact that I didn't yet speak enough French to comprehend the chattering of those around me was also very comforting. I had decided to treat myself to an evening in the Latin Quarter, and so, finishing my drink, I headed for the Metro.

My friend Eleanor had suggested I stop by the Cloister, a wine bar on Rue St. Jacques, just around the corner from the famous bookstore, *Shakespeare and Co.* Eleanor had graduated from UCLA the year before with a BFA in dance and had been in Paris ever since, trying to break into the ballet scene. It was she who had introduced me to Fabrice's father for the job that would be short lived.

I went first into the bookstore, where I found myself enthralled by the lingering vibrations of the great artists and poets who had hung out there: Picasso, Braque, Baudelaire, Verlaine, and my beloved Rimbaud. I climbed the stairs to the small apartment where writers of every sort had often been allowed to take shelter for a time and rested a while in a large, ancient, overstuffed wingback chair. Then I made my way back downstairs and out, around the corner to the Cloister. The front was all French windowpanes, neatly wood framed. I was surprised to find that the inside was done in Tudor style. I sat at the bar alone and ordered a glass of white wine.

Quickly after the first few sips, I saw him. His shoulder-length hair was clean, though slightly unkempt, and he wore an olive-green army fatigue jacket. I knew immediately he felt me by the way he purposely avoided looking at me as he sauntered over to an apparently arbitrary seat at a table near the bar. He ordered a drink continuing to pretend I wasn't there as I watched him with great intent out of the corner of my eye.

Then I looked away entirely and gave my full attention to feeling him, as if within me. I had learned in my experimental theatre classes how to send a message without speaking or gesturing in any way, how to direct a feeling to touch someone across a room, and to manipulate energy as well as the color of its radiance.

So I decided to practice. I chose the color red and imagined that the energy was flowing down from my hips to the floor and running along like a stream to his feet and up his legs. I know he felt it. I felt him try to shake it off and was surprised when he got up abruptly and walked out the door. Of course, I followed him out and down the sidewalk, staying ten or twenty paces behind, walking through the streets and into a darkened alley.

When even then I did not leave, he finally turned around and asked, "Mais, qu'est-ce que tu veux?" ("But what do you want?")

"Je veux toi," ("I want you,") I retorted boldly.

He turned away, shrugging his shoulders as if to say, "So come along if you cannot be dissuaded."

I quickened my step to catch up and walk beside him. The first recognition was how our gait matched, pace by pace, step by swift step, we began our march through the night streets of Paris, in perfect unison.

After several blocks in silence, he casually asked, "So what are you doing here in Paris?" His voice was deep and rich, its warm tone slipping through his soft accent, belied the disinterest he still attempted to feign.

"I'm here to learn French."

He rolled his eyes.

"I'm on my way to Grotowski's Theatre Laboratorium in Wrocław, Poland. The stipulation is that all participants speak French. Thank God he's not insisting on Polish!" Now he was intrigued, and so it was that Jean and I, began our night walk throughout Paris.

Jean took me on an amazing tour that would continue until dawn. He knew Paris like a kid knows his own backyard, and Paris knew him. He led me into the corners and

4

alcoves where the poor hid from "les flics" rather than be herded up and hauled outside Paris each night, as they were, to prevent them from sleeping in the streets.

We came upon a group gathered around several crates of grapes. Jean whispered, "They've stolen these." And as we continued to approach them, he asked quietly, "Are you afraid?"

"No," I responded simply, already knowing I would follow him anywhere.

We joined them, and they shared their grapes with us. They knew Jean; this was not the first time they'd met him. He was welcomed and trusted.

We had our fill and moved on. I asked a little about his family. He was an only child, given up by his mother at birth. She tossed him into the arms of his father, who took him to be raised by his grandmother. He revealed it all without a single trace of emotion.

We continued on tirelessly through the streets. It was already the best adventure I'd had in some time. With my insatiable passion for life, I was enthralled by the magic of our meeting and the energy it filled us with.

As dawn approached, he asked where I lived and began leading us towards my place. I took him up to my tiny, humble servant's quarters and grabbed my camera. I was about to take a picture of him when he said, "Come," and led me out of my room and up to the rooftop. Now all of Paris was laid at my feet, and he photographed me as I skipped and danced in the sweet dawn's light. Then abruptly he announced it was time for him to leave.

I went with him back down to the street, kissed him on both cheeks, embraced him warmly, and looking into his eyes asked, "Where will I find you again?"

He puffed up his cheeks, blew the air out, shook his head, shrugged his shoulders, and said, "Ch'sais pas" ("I don't know when").

I let him go without another word.

Somehow, I slept and upon awakening I realized I had to see him again, but how? Oddly enough, that day Fabrice's father made a pass at me, and I resigned. This, of course, meant that I'd have to find a new position and hence new lodgings. Now how would Jean find me or I him?

I realized there was only one chance; return to the Cloister again that night, around the same time and wait to see if he shows up. So I did. I arrived around 8 pm, sat alone at the bar, and waited. I was sure he'd come. I glanced occasionally at the door, each time expecting he'd be the next to open it. At 10 pm I left, slightly dismayed, but vowing to return the next night.

After several nights of fruitless waiting, my friend Robyn and her boyfriend, Andre asked me to join them for a late night of partying. I agreed to go with them only on the condition that we meet at the Cloister and wait for Jean to come, or until I was ready to leave. Jean did not show up, and after a few rolled eyes and exasperated sighs from Robyn, I agreed to leave with them for a nightclub that was in an underground cave-like structure.

Robyn and I were fairly new friends. She had jumped onto the Grotowski train at the last minute. Her parents were willing and able to support her every whim, whereas I had worked two jobs day and night while attending classes just to get to Paris to study French. I would still have to wait for an invitation from the Theatre Lab and then go for a final interview before, hopefully, being accepted into the

"Rencontres Preliminaires". I wasn't terribly close to her, probably because she arrived at a time when I was entirely wrapped up in my own journey, though she did seem somewhat enamored of me. She was a beautiful, wild girl, hungry for adventure, fiery, independent, full of life and passion.

Something strange and new happened that night between us, granted we'd had quite a few drinks. We brushed by one another in a narrow hallway of the cave and suddenly found ourselves frozen in a moment of time. Our eyes locked in a deep gaze. I felt a titillating rush of warmth and then we kissed. Smiling and laughing like children, we said, "Let's get Andre!"

Andre was a French-born Arab, whose father was out of the home. So feeling responsible to take care of his mother, he was running hash out of Amsterdam as a profession. In his next run he would be captured and imprisoned. Apparently, the police had become aware of his dealings. How sad...so often an individual, desperate to raise their station in life and believing money will do it, is willing to risk their freedom to get it.

Later, we all wound up on the mattress in my shoddy little room, until Robyn froze up and realized it was not what she wanted. She left abruptly before anything really happened, with Andre following swiftly behind her. I was relieved, seeing that the fantasy is far sweeter than the reality, where one must deal with the feelings of others, and the emotions of women are more than I can handle.

In the morning I went over to the Alliance Française, where I was supposedly studying French, and checked the job board. I found another au pair position in the 16th District with Madame G de la-- and her husband Monsieur.

Madame was German born. Her father was a doctor in Germany, who in 1939 decided wisely to move his entire family to the States, sending Madame to Switzerland to complete her education. There, towards the end of the war, she would meet her French Lieutenant and marry him. She was quick to tell me that he was no longer entitled to his "de la" as the land had long ago been sold, and the aristocratic position lost with it.

I arrived at Madame's door unannounced to ask for the job, and she later told me, "Whenever you are looking for work, don't call, just arrive at the door as you did here. Your face convinced me to hire you. Had you called, and I knew you were American, I would not have considered you."

I believe I held myself back from saying, "Had I known you were German, I would not have come."

Silently, I realized how glad I was to be there with her and how oddly that thought struck me. My parents told us that we were three -quarters Irish and one-quarter German, when in fact the Irish blood was topped off with Polish. I was only casually told the truth by my mother when I announced that I intended to go and study in Poland.

Interesting how coolly parents can lie to their children when they believe they have good reason. Unknown as yet to either of them, the Polish blood was Jewish, being passed through my mother's side making her, as well as all her Catholic-born children, Jews. A fact I would discover some twelve years later. I was tormented by memories of atrocities from a war before my time, memories I should not have been able to recall, but somehow did. Too often those nightmares broke through my dreams, and I was not yet sure why.

Madame was an intelligent woman, speaking three languages perfectly: German, French, and English. I have her to thank for whatever French I speak. She never failed to correct my mistakes, and I regarded this as a form of respect rather than a taunt or an insult. On the contrary, I regard the refusal of friends to bother correcting my mistakes in other languages as a form of disrespect. She was extremely kind to me despite our vast differences.

I remember telling her once, upon completing a task, "Je suis finie." ("I am finished.")

To which she replied, "A vingt et un tu n'es pas finie! On dis: 'J'ai finie'." ("At twenty-one you are not finished! One says, 'I have finished.'")

I was given a wonderful room on the top floor servant's quarters. It was a small place, though not confining. There was an antique wood-burning heater, an ample and comfortable bed with attractive spreads, and beautiful wood floors worn by the feet of a century's servants and covered with a once-fine area rug. A sink was in the corner near the footboard of the bed, with a bowl and pitcher on the counter. I was expected to use that to wash, except for the two days a week when Madame allowed me to use her bathtub after work. I became an expert at cat baths.

Daylight would fill the room through a slightly slanted window that offered me a delightful view of Paris. Since Madame's exquisite home was on the 7th floor, a small wooden staircase connected my room directly to her kitchen door.

My day at Madame's began at 8 am. I entered by the kitchen door, where a small plate of cheese, butter, and a few slices of a fresh baguette with a cup of coffee would be waiting for me. I would sit there quietly and finish the delightful petit déjeuner she'd prepared for me. Then work began. I cleaned the house, ironed, and on the rare occasions when I was a little ill, Madame would sit me by a window to sew, and I would drink fennel tea all morning.

She was all at once stern and kind. It would be years before I realized how much I loved and valued her. At noon each day I would join her in the kitchen to prepare the lunch. I began cooking with my mother at a very early age and was delighted to learn new dishes from Madame: cheese fondue, leek soup, rabbit in red wine, and many more. I did find the blutwurst disgusting to look at but delicious to eat.

We lunched all together in the dining room. I learned how to set the table for a king, as well as aristocratic table manners, including the importance of folding your napkin exactly as you found it and pushing your chair in each and every time you leave the table.

Madame was constantly harping on to Monsieur about his table manners. "Prends ta serviette!" ("Use your napkin!") "Ne coupes pas ta viande avant de la manger!" ("Don't cut your meat before you eat it!")

Once she warned me, "Never marry an older man, because in the beginning you're his daughter and at the end you're his nurse."

Every evening, I'd take the short walk up Theophile Gautier, the street where I lived, to Metro Église d'Auteuil. Heading to Rue St. Jacques, just across the Seine from Notre Dame, I went back into the Cloister to wait for Jean. Night after night I returned to wait for him. From 8 pm until at least 10 pm, I sat alone, usually at the bar. In the beginning of my vigil for Jean, I knew he would come eventually. As the nights of waiting wore on, I began to doubt, but I refused to give up, until that one night, when I told myself, "This is the last time I'll wait for him."

Sure enough, that night the door opened, and at long last, it was Jean! He strode straight toward me and sat down assuredly next to me. My heart was leaping for joy inside, but I regarded him slightly sternly and said, "I've been here every night waiting for you, alone."

"Except for one night," he responded.

Immediately I understood. He must have come every night, peered into the windows, and gone on, unable to find the courage to come in. I never made him admit that. He was here now, and I loved him. He told me he had gone back and left a note on the door at Rue Delambre. I explained to him that I had changed lodgings and was now living at 60 Theophile Gautier. Jean laughed out loud.

"What?" I asked him somewhat puzzled.

"I live a few houses down the same street!"

"C'est pas vrai?" ("This can't be true?")

"No, c'est vrai." ("No, it is true.")

We left the Cloister and returned to our neighborhood together.

It always amused me that we met at the Cloister. I had come very close to becoming a cloistered nun, as was my early childhood desire and intent. I awoke in this life with a bizarre sensation that my soul was somehow in danger. It was as if I felt from the beginning that there was some history I needed to pay for, to pray for my soul. True, being raised by a devout Catholic might have brought about such feelings in many, but for me it was clearly present before I knew the dogma. I knew there was something I needed to know, to live, and I began begging for it early on.

One Sunday morning after Mass, when I was five, I went to my well-meaning parents and said, "I need to ask you something."

They could see I was earnest and accompanied me into the living room of our home in Buffalo, New York, sitting to either side of me on the sofa.

"I need to know what love is. What is it?" I asked, intently serious.

"Oh," they responded simultaneously as if pained by the question. "We love you. Don't you know we love you?"

"Yes, I know you love me, but I need to know what Love is!"

They each reached out to give me a little hug saying, "Now don't be silly, you know we love you!"

I realized that either they had not understood the question or they did not know the answer. The subject was dismissed, and I went back to begging a God I wasn't at all sure even existed for answers.

I used to take off my precious little turquoise ring that was a gift from my father and place it on the bureau each night, asking God to take it, explaining to myself that if it was gone in the morning, I would know that He existed and therefore might one day answer my prayer. Every morning I was dismayed to find it was still there.

By the time I was six we had moved to Penfield, New York. Our home was surrounded by a forest, in which I took comfort on many solitary walks. My imagination always flourishing, I gave names to the branches of trees. The frogs became my friends, and I could cross the creek dancing over mossy rocks without slipping. There, beneath the leaves rustling in a breeze, perhaps generated by the flapping wings of angels and surrounded by so much beauty, I longed for more. I wandered along the paths that wound through the woods as if searching for that missing peace I prayed for.

My father, aside from being an extremely handsome man, a fact agreed upon by absolutely everyone, was deeply religious and a theologian in his own right. He was unaware of my lack of faith, as I hid it from him well. I was devoted to him and anxious for his approval. Mother, bless her heart, was very pretty however not the least bit religious, though she too hid it well and sometimes referred to me as the "religious one" with just a trace of sarcasm.

I attended Catholic School, cleaned the church with the nuns on Saturday rather than watch cartoons, and sang in the choir for two masses on Sundays. I made a study of the cloisters, reading *The Story of a Soul*, the autobiography of St. Therese of Lisieux. I began to model my life after her, committed to entering the Cloister as early as possible, like she did, at twelve.

My teacher, Sister Marie, in response to me professing my vocation, said, "You will never enter the Convent." It was as if she had stepped on my heart. I was crushed.

"What do mean? Why do you say that? How could you know?" I asked frantically.

"I can tell by the way you walk," she replied gently, though with conviction. "You walk as if you're going somewhere."

Not to be dissuaded, I continued to behave as if I were part of the Sisterhood, marching around in a circle through the snow, missal in hand, praying. Often at night I would sit with my father until very late, engaged in intense theological discussions.

It was the day that President Kennedy was shot and my little brother Joseph's birthday, a day of shock and tears for everyone, even the children. Mother had somehow managed to make a small celebration for Joe, nonetheless. That evening my father arrived home late, long after the candles had been blown out on Joe's cake. He came through the front door with a large gift under his arm for Joseph, which was unusual, as it was Mother who normally bought the presents. Mother seemed worried more than angry. He was at least a little tipsy, almost too cheerful. Of course, I can imagine half the country was getting drunk that night and likely all the Irish. No excuse.

The other children had already gone upstairs with Mother to get ready for bed when I went into the living room to kiss him good night. I could see that he was sad. We were moving to California soon. I was wearing my pajamas and a robe, as he required of my sister Kate and me whenever we were roaming around the house at night. My brothers could walk around in their boxers with their "junk" bouncing, no matter. Suddenly he pretended to dance with me, swinging me around, and then I felt his arms slip into my robe. I was frightened as he stroked my back and terrified when he reached around cupping my breasts, touching my nipples with his fingertips. My heart raced as my stomach churned. A sickening feeling filled the air. I pushed him away and ran upstairs. It would be decades before I ever had any feeling in my breasts again.

He had told me he was pious, made me believe he was a saint, and now he had desecrated me. My heart filled with hate as I fell upon my knees and prayed to a God that I now loathed for leaving me in the hands of one who could so destroy my trust in love.

14

I got up off my knees, went into the bathroom, grabbed a bottle of Lavoris mouthwash and took a swig as if it was whiskey. Then I went into my parent's room, where both he and my mother were sound asleep. I walked around to his side of the bed, stood over him, and shook my fist at him in the dark silence. I was only 11 years old.

I went to school the next morning with my brothers and sister. I tried to hold it together until mid-morning when the sick feeling inside became unbearable, and I could hardly hold back the tears. For the first time ever, I asked to be excused from class. I was sent to the principal's office, weeping uncontrollably by the time I got there. I explained that I was feeling terribly ill. She was obviously concerned by my condition and called my mother to come and get me.

I told my mother in the car on the way home. Her concern was touching, and I am sure it was difficult for her to contain herself. It would take a little time for the shock to wear off, to be followed by anger, fury, rage, and ultimately a devastating helplessness. She had six children with him, and he was about to uproot the entire family and move us to California. Later that day she came to me saying she asked him about it and he said it was nothing, no different than hugging Joseph. I glared at her and turned away. We both knew that was a lie.

I cried every day, all the way across the country. Only he and Mother knew why. I was eleven years old. It is my confronting nature that has inevitably saved me from the life of an eternal victim. When I was 17, I charged at him in the kitchen of their home. I had moved out a few months earlier. He had tried to stop me from leaving by physically blocking the front door, but my younger brother John came up, to my surprise, and threatened to deck him if he wouldn't get out of my way. He could not really have been afraid of John, because he was strong enough to take on any of his four sons. So he must have suddenly realized he had to let me go. Still, I have always been grateful to John for the courage he showed in that moment.

Mother sat silently by, no doubt numb with despair. Why had I not forgotten about it as she had pleaded with me to do so long ago and why was I bringing it up now?

My Father squirmed and cringed inside as I ranted on, forcing him to remember that horrible night. Finally, I declared, "Because of you, I will never be a normal woman!"

Just then, we saw my sister Kate and her husband coming up the walkway to join us for dinner. By then my father was weeping copiously, so we slipped into the laundry room together. He was shaking uncontrollably from head to toe when he reached out to gently wrap his arms around my shoulders and begged my forgiveness. I could feel his contrition in the marrow of my bones, and so I readily forgave him, hence saving myself.

*

Jean followed me through the servant's door, up the spiral wooden staircase to the eighth-floor servant's quarters and into my small room. He peeled off his combat jacket, hanging it carefully over the only chair, and looking around kindly, he said, "It's nice."

"I know. I like it."

Without another word Jean picked up a few logs and started a fire in the stove for us. Then he kissed me, so deep and so warm that my knees went weak as I melted into his embrace. At last, he was in my arms. God, how I loved him.

His wonderful strong hands caressed me with such tenderness. Hesitating just a little at each moment as if asking for permission to go on, he slipped his hands under my blouse and explored every vertebra, every rib, my scapulae, and my waist. Then he cupped his hands over my breasts, and I gasped as he gingerly began unbuttoning my blouse.

Softly laying me upon my bed, Jean delighted in every inch of my flesh, as a rush of sweet tenderness began filling my blood like wine. Our bodies sculpted against one another in the beautiful living art form only great lovers know. I slid down his chest caressing him with my breasts and wrapped him in my mouth as he moaned. He drew me back up to him and spread my legs, pausing a moment to look, before taking that first lick of the pure honey-like fluid that seeped from within me. My increasing excitement amplified his arousal, and when he finally entered me, I was instantly in ecstasy. Rarely in my life have I known anyone who could match my passion. Jean would always remain among the few.

As I lay spent in his arms, melting like snow under the sun, I whispered to him, "You are a wonderful lover!" He let out a barely audible little chuckle.

"What?" I asked.

"Oh, nothing." Then after a second's silence, "You are my first—woman, that is." I made no remark, though he must have sensed I was curious.

"I was with a boy once—a year and a half ago. He was seventeen."

I kissed his shoulder, ever so gently, placed my head upon his chest, and went to sleep, treasuring him with all my heart.

Chapter Two — Spark

I wasn't aware of being pretty; I was aware of not being pretty enough. My sister Kate was the blonde, beautiful one, and everyone remarked about it in front of me, unabashedly, all the time. My singing voice though was absolutely exquisite and just a mark over hers, so the family comforted me with that ranking. Kate, however, played Chopin like Brailowsky, and I could weep from the beauty as she practiced the "Etudes".

I entered high school, fully intending to devote myself entirely to my studies. So imagine my surprise when the boys started coming after me! I was standing by my locker when Rupert came along. He was a handsome young lad in a letterman's jacket (and would later confess that he'd been trying to get the courage up to ask me to homecoming for days). He was always a perfect gentleman and very good at planning dates.

We rode his Yamaha over the dirt paths of the hills that surrounded our homes and into the hidden forests. Sometimes he would borrow his father's beautiful dark blue Cadillac with a white vinyl roof and plenty of room to play.

Once, we went up to the mountains in winter. He brought a loaf of French bread, sliced rare roast beef, and cheese. We spent the afternoon sitting in the car making sandwiches and kissing as the snow kept falling all around us. It was sweet. Another time he took me to Philippe's in L.A. just to have their "French Dipped Sandwich." And of course, we went to that homecoming and the Christmas Ball, all the things you're supposed to do with a boyfriend and then some.

We began holding hands. His hands were rough and calloused from swinging on the high bar. He was an exceptional gymnast and ultimately became captain of the team. We kissed as kids do and started making out parked on the hillside overlooking our town. We came in one another's hands. I was shocked the first time I saw his cum.

"What's that?"

"It's the sperm," he explained gently. "It's normal. It comes out when a man comes."

Talk about sheltered! I didn't know what a wet dream was until I was 25. It was all wonderfully new and exciting, though we never went all the way.

Having a boyfriend to hold my hand across campus was comforting for me. I used to walk as closely as possible to the walls of the exterior corridors to avoid rubbing shoulders with the masses rushing to their next classes. I have never been able to stand comfortably in a crowd without being engulfed by their anxiety, as well as my own. My nerves have always been too close to the surface. I am like a sponge in water, soaking up the emotions of those around me. Later, after years of study in ancient and avant-garde theater techniques, I would gain some control over this but never be completely free of it.

Rupert truly cherished me, and I cared for him. I enjoyed his attention and respect. Even though later I would hurt him, somehow, we would remain friends. And many years later, after my first sabbatical in Europe, I would find him sitting waiting for me at my front door in Hollywood.

He had a beard, and his hair was long and scraggly. I was extremely surprised to see him and even more surprised to know why he had come. I invited him up to my flat, a section of a wonderful old Spanish home that had been partitioned off into several apartments. Mine was at the front. A large stained-glass window let light pour in through the downstairs entryway. My large single room was up a flight of terra-cotta stairs, had wood floors and eight-foot French windows overlooking the side scrubs. There was a small but complete bathroom and a tiny kitchen where I made many delicious feasts for my friends.

Rupert was a UCLA graduate, and now he sat across the room from me looking nervous. "I've bought land in Oxnard. I intend to farm it and I've come here to ask you to be my wife."

My jaw may have actually dropped. I was in shock, but grateful to know that he seemed to have forgiven me for hurting him. I was so sorry that I had to hurt him again by saying, "No." I was so far beyond any such possibility. But after that I never saw or heard from him again.

Spring came early in my freshman year and the blossoms began to burst forth from the tips of young trees scattered around the modern campus of South Hills High School.

Light refracted through the windows of the round cafeteria building. I had a large square slice of memorably rich chocolate cake and washed it down with milk, grateful to be alone in the nearly empty spacious room.

Then suddenly the doors swung wide open, and in walked a tall thin boy, taking long steady strides towards me. It was Spark, the side-horse man on Rupert's gymnastic team. He plopped himself down on the bench just across from me, placing a black-and-white speckled composition book on the table in front of him. He looked at me deeply with his sky-blue eyes, taking in a full breath as he smiled at me broadly. I was already charmed.

"Aren't you Rupert's girlfriend?" he asked as if he didn't know.

"Yes," I answered strangely indefinitely.

"I want to read you something I wrote."

"Okay," I said cautiously.

He read me a poem he would later turn into a song:

There is a time when you find
that you can't change your mind
when you know that it's too late
to hold what's behind you
you might say, 'not today'
if you could change your way
but you took that one step
and it's too late to stay
still it's only the now
in between why and how
that you stand so afraid
of the changes you've made.

Don't let years bring you tears
and forget all your fears
it's just before you start
that your mind is so unclear

try to smile and beguile
you will find in a while
it's not very far
though it may seem like miles
soon the changes to show
you what way is best to go
it's just before you start
you think you'll fall apart.

"I love it," I remarked a little casually, though quite sincerely. It inspired me to respond with poetry, and soon we were meeting each day, reading our poems together. It was our way of sharing our feelings with each other. We sat together talking for hours. It was truly as if I'd never spoken with anyone before, like I had been cloistered forever and now I could speak and be heard, and I could hear him. It was such a relief to me. His eyes always glistened when he looked at me, and I was totally enthralled with him, so sweet and pure. I knew I loved him, but that frightened me. It required trust to allow myself to love, but that ability was still broken in me. He had no way of knowing. I would have told him if only I had known the consequence of the secret I bore and what it would do to us.

*

Spark was extremely kind and patient with me. He agreed to wait a while for me to confess my true feelings to Rupert and break up with him. I decided I should wait until June, when the school year would be over and he would suffer the least amount of embarrassment. Spark bought that because he trusted and believed in the wonderful feeling he was wrapped in. Truthfully, I was just buying time for myself to gather the courage to abandon all my reluctance and fears, so I could finally give myself to him.

Spark was the youngest of nine children. The eight preceding him were highly educated and successful, with impressive titles. Spark also had a voracious appetite for knowledge, but his studies were driven by his current interests and his desire to educate himself, not for acclaim or approval from the world. I respected and admired him deeply, as I too lived outside the world.

We continued to spend as much time as possible together. Rupert must have felt my attention drifting, but he bought the idea that Spark and I were just friends. He was certainly unaware how deeply in love I had become with Spark. I still felt safe with Rupert. There was no risk.

I attended the gymnastic meets and openly rooted for both men, since they each excelled on a different apparatus. Rupert was on the high bar and the rings. Spark was on the side-horse primarily. Because of his long lanky form, he looked like a giant graceful bird, flying around, swinging back and forth over and off of it. I really enjoyed watching them; they were both beautiful.

Sometimes at school Spark and I went into the music building hoping to find an open practice room with a piano, so he could play for me. He played well, singing his own songs as well as Dylan's. Their voices were somewhat similar. Music would always be an easy avenue to reach me, especially on piano.

Spark didn't have a car or a motorcycle, so we hitchhiked everywhere we went, often ditching classes to head up into the hills that were the backdrop of the school. I enjoyed climbing to the top and looking out over the valleys below because of the way it made everything appear small, like I was above it all. The breeze brushed the tall dried grasses, making cushions for us.

I could sit for hours and listen to him tell me all about the latest discovery in his self-directed studies. True he was a schoolboy in love, but he was a genius and would forever be a student. I loved his enthusiasm, the way he could always challenge me to go further into the woods, climb higher up to the hilltops, and jump 12-foot fences topped with barbed wire. Like the ones we encountered in the back perimeters of the Claremont Colleges, after we searched Sproul Hall unsuccessfully for a piano, then went instead to wander through the orange groves. At times, his long-fingered hands entwined in mine and his great arms held me gently against his skinny body. For only a moment, I was sure I'd never be alone again.

Summer solstice was fast approaching, the day I'd promised Spark that I would finally be his. It was evening as I sat alone in my room, the smell of my sister Kate's *Intimate* cologne wafting from the scent-drenched clothes in our closet. I was writing in my journal, musing over my impending decision, when my father called down the hall for me, "Someone is here to see you."

I headed to the front door where my father stood. I was pleased to see that it was Spark waiting for me. His hair was untrimmed. He wore a simple white t-shirt and well-worn jeans, tightly belted to prevent them from slipping down his bony hips.

My father stopped me at the threshold to ask, "Do you go out looking for these people or do they just find you?"

I walked by him, ignoring that, and ran up to Spark throwing my arms around him. He had something in his hand. "Here, I made something for you."

It was an 8 x 11 piece of white poster board on which he had used pen and ink to inscribe a new poem for me. Beneath the words he'd inked a simple, artful gate, slightly broken. It read:

"Do what you will I'll be here
waiting still that time of year
when the leaves of late were green
kissed with love no longer seen
when the heat stays late at night
and the days are strained with light
then stopping by your back gate
hoping that it is not too late
I'll wait a while hoping still for your smile
and that it will be all that you said
that's been ringing head
that's been with me day and night
all I see in every sight
all I hear in every song
all I've been so very long."

"It's beautiful," I said, wiping away a tear, silently disturbed by the broken gate at the bottom. Did he know...?

On the summer solstice we met and hitchhiked out to our favorite spot behind the Claremont Colleges. I could feel Spark's glee in every step. He was a man now, and as we stood in the dirt of the orange grove on the other side of the high chain link fence we'd just jumped, he placed his hands on my shoulders looking deeply into my eyes, as his beautiful big sky-blue eyes widened, and gently placed his lips upon mine.

One day I would learn, it was his first kiss. He had saved it for me. I drew back with a little smile and told him I could not stay with him. I was scared. My trust in love had been destroyed long ago. On our way back, his eyes were filled with tears. I don't know how he prevented them from falling. He dropped me off at home and turned away without a word.

Immediately I regretted my stupidity, and within a day I went searching for him. Someone told me he was hanging out in an abandoned church across from Covina Park. I headed out to find him. I was surprised to find the old White Church filled with hippies sitting on the floor, smoking pot and sharing poetry as if it was Berkeley.

Spark was the star with his guitar. He seemed all at once surprised and disinterested to see me. I asked him to come outside to speak with me. Reluctantly, he did.

On the sidewalk I said, "I'm sorry, I love you. I really do."

He glared at me. "You are incapable of love!" he roared and turned away, heading back into the church.

I was aghast. The only one who ever knew me, the only one whose opinion mattered, the only one I trusted, declared me incapable of loving. How could he say that to me? I had to believe, after arduous consideration, that it must be true.

I went home and looked for a while at myself in the mirror. I recalled the scene in Camelot where Guinevere and Arthur stand together in the woods, saying goodbye before she leaves for the nunnery and she cuts her hair off, dropping it on the forest floor. I drew my hair back, still staring into the glass, gathered it at the nape of my neck, picked up the scissors and chopped it off with one cut. Luckily it came out looking like the then famous Sassoon horseshoe style, very cute.

How could I have known that some horrible, jealous brat of a girl named Linda had told him, for her own insidious purposes, that I had had intercourse with Rupert. It wasn't true, but he must have been so mortified and disgusted, he couldn't even bear to accuse me. Surely that was the reason I turned from him, he must have thought. I never returned to Rupert, and the part of me that belonged to Spark would remain alone for the rest of my life.

I wouldn't even know what had happened until nearly forty years later when he tossed it out casually on the table at a Pakistani restaurant in Berkeley where we sat with a couple of my dear friends, Ronnie and Jon. I was stunned. I could hardly believe my ears.

"It's not true, Spark," I said, touching his elbow. "I never had sex with him!" He sloughed it off as if it didn't matter now. "It never happened!" I declared again, emphatically, but then I saw in his face that he could hardly bear to hear me let alone believe me. That lie had turned the tide of both our lives, and there was nothing to be done about it now, the stuff Shakespeare's tragedies are made of.

In the morning mist, I sat beneath the bell tower that housed a magnificent organ and listened to an anonymous soul pound out "Trumpet Voluntary" brilliantly. Kate was a new resident of the so-called Virgin Hill at UC Riverside, and my parents had become used to allowing me extreme latitude, so my request to spend two weeks on sabbatical from my sophomore year and visit Kate was granted. Perhaps they noticed I was beginning to slide off the edge.

I spent almost all my time alone anyway, writing copious journals or hiding behind the library stacks, reading and researching. I read Camus and casually contemplated suicide (though never seriously considered it). My Catholic education stood for something, and I couldn't take the risk of eternal damnation on top of everything else! I read once that dentists were most likely to do it, followed by psychiatrists and then waitresses.

At UCR I audited classes, a practice I would find most appealing later on, as it allowed me to wander into any lectures I wished to, learn whenever I wanted to, and move on, accountable to no one. Besides I suffered from severe claustrophobia and could hardly bear crowded classrooms. I had to sit either in the front row of those classes or the very back when I wasn't sure I wanted to stay, so I could escape easily. I recall attending a lecture on Kant and Anselm, as well as one on Pasternak, popular then because the film Dr. Zhivago was out. I had just seen it, and strangely enough, many years later I would have a wonderful affair with one of its major stars.

I remember sitting back against the trunk of a willow, always one of my very favorite trees because I was hidden beneath it, and I wrote this poem to Spark long after he could hear it or care.

The Promethean Poet

In a time before morning
watching children's toys play
I sat sadly longing
for some lost fated day
when the promethean poet
would come again this way.

In the cobbled streets of town,
the water droplets play
and a fire waits to warm me
asking me to stay
but as my book lies open
there are roads I still must take
finding as I look around
I'm finally awake
and tripping along the hillside
I hoped for that day
when the promethean poet
would come again this way.

I remember my friend and I
amid the wind god's breeze
reading poems in the land
running through willow trees
Love, bathing hands with his touch,
begged me to come that way
but drenched in fears of being lost
I turned and rode away

And at the last of each day
knelt on cushions of velvet, she prays
for only a glimpse
of the lost fated day
when the promethean poet
would come again this way.

The following year I became more creative with my own destruction and began starving myself. The year before, I'd started studying psychology and philosophy, to no avail. I found some small measure of peace working out routines on the balancing beam. It helped me feel in control and so somehow free. I realized I could do whatever I wanted.

I wrote of my travels through a dangerous life, or at least a somewhat reckless one. I remember that summer before my junior year, when I somehow convinced my father that I would have to stay behind to work while the family went on vacation to San Diego. Actually, the second after I finished waving at their car vanishing down the road, I stuck my thumb out and headed for Isla Vista. I.V. was a student housing area of UC Santa Barbara, visited by many pot-smoking hippies.

I was not smoking pot at that time. I was a virgin traveler, with only my journal in hand and my wit to guide me. I developed relationships with people as I went along my way and I recorded my impression of them with unvarnished insight. I was fascinated by the intense, though brief, encounters I could have with strangers rather than hoping to develop more enduring relationships.

In a fleeting thought, it occurred to me that it wasn't fair, my parents not knowing where I was. Still I was searching for something solid, and having no idea where

I'd find it, I was willing to look everywhere. I spent that night in the sleeping bag I'd brought with me under a tree behind a stranger's house on a bluff overlooking the sea.

I made it back home the next day, in time to make dinner for my little brother Joe and for my parents to find me there with him, unaware of my adventure.

I can't say the same about my first mescaline trip. I would have to let them believe I'd lost my virginity rather than have them think I'd gone insane and possibly put me away.

It was November 15, 1969, the day of the moratorium march to end the war in Vietnam, in San Francisco. I climbed into the back of a van headed up to S.F. with a bunch of Rupert's friends from UCLA. Driving into S.F. looking out the back window of a van was a really bad way to view a city. I was going with them not as a protester, merely as an observer of mass movements. I had already read Eric Hoffer's True Believer and was certain that no revolution ever achieved its purist goal because there were always too many people turning the tide of the group for their own private desires.

So though I submitted to wearing a black armband for the dead once we got there, I felt trapped. Half-blinded by the encompassing crowd, I literally stood on the sidelines, moving along with the marchers, as I watched from the sidewalk. Though I believed the demonstration must have succeeded in impressing the nation, I still could not relate.

The march was followed by a concert and a love-in, a concept I considered absurd and annoying. Love-in what? Besides I could not stand in a crowd of strangers, body bumping against body. My parents only briefly crossed my mind as passive images, irrelevant to my present state. They had no idea where I was.

Later that night, we all went to a friend's apartment to crash on whatever couch or floor we could find. I had been speaking with an archaeology student I found interesting. He was aware of my age, so nothing would come of it except for a mescaline connection. He told me that he had a powerful spiritual experience when he took it and was inspired to try it because the Native American tribes used it in their rituals. I was determined to experience everything I could, without harming anyone else. And I supposed perhaps there could be some trick to it, that one had to take something to know the Truth.

I took the five large brown pills that were offered to me and packed them away carefully in a small matchbox, for a time in the near future. The next week I talked it over with my friend David, who said he'd like to drop it with me.

David was the nephew of one of the nation's most famous ad men, and he was himself a fine actor from another high school who had sought me out after seeing my sophomore performance of Mary Warren in the "Crucible."

My mother had also seen it and commented, "I didn't like seeing you that way. I didn't recognize you!" Yes Mother, as an actor, I would interlope my way across the world.

David had expressed his admiration for me saying, "Of course, I am in love with you, how could I not be? But I know I don't have a chance. Still I must have you there when I die. Promise me you'll come to my deathbed, for I cannot die without you." His passion was emphasized by his deep rich voice, and I agreed to fly to his side when he was ready to die. Just recently I discovered he has been dead for ten years. I wish he had called me.

We did, however, plan to drop the mescaline together the following weekend. I had never even smoked a joint before, so David brought some hash with him to start me off. We met near the park. I left my 1959 black Buick parked, jumped into his car and off we went on a drive through the hills.

I opened the matchbox and stared at the pills within. "What will happen if I take this?"

"Well, here, try this first." He passed me a pipe filled with hash. I took a toke; it seemed okay.

"So what *will* it be like if I take one of these?"

"Well," he said reaching for words, "it'll be like this, only much more intense." As if I could imagine what that meant! I took it before David could tell me he'd changed his mind and would have to be getting home now.

I had told my parents, once again, that I'd be at Linda's house. David dropped me off at my car and left me there, a novice coming on to a powerful psychedelic, alone.

There was only one person who I knew could help me, Spark. He was then attending classes at Claremont Colleges and living out there as well. I knew the name of the street and approximately where it was, but I would have to drive there via the freeway while seeing quadruple! I aimed my car between the two middle sets of the four taillights I was seeing on the car ahead of me. It was surely one the most terrifying times in my life, but I had to get to Spark.

By the time I pulled off the freeway and began to search for his street, I could barely see the street signs, let alone read them. Between the streaming lights and the gathering fog, what magnet drew me to him with unwavering protection? I will never know exactly how I survived that drive or how I happened upon his house, but when he flung open the door, I was all at once stunned and grateful—stunned to have actually found him and grateful to the strange and wonderful protective force that took me there safely.

He wrapped his arms around me for just a moment. Then he sat me down on the sofa and sat on the couch across from me. He offered what was always his nature—to be kind and gentle. He listened as I told him what I'd done and he talked me down a little, explaining exactly what was coming next and how best to get through it. I felt ashamed to have come to him in this condition—so helpless yet so grateful he was there.

Spark had been experimenting with psychedelics for some time, often fasting for three days and then dropping three windowpanes of Grateful Dead acid at once! I can't imagine. The suffering I went through in my mind that night took all my strength to hold onto my sanity! I closed my eyes and saw endless geometric patterns moving across dome ceilings. It wasn't so much the hallucinations as the fact that I could not control them.

I opened my eyes to make the visions stop and saw Spark laying on the sofa across the room from me with his penis standing straight up a foot high out of his jeans. Surely, I was still hallucinating? He must have thought I was asleep, as I closed my eyes and pretended to be. He did not approach me.

By dawn I was fully awake, and before anyone else woke, I crept out. I drove out to Riverside and ended my trip dancing in the dew beneath my beloved bell tower while the anonymous organist played Vivaldi's "The Four Seasons."

A photographer from Santa Barbara happened to be there taking pictures of the tower and asked if he could photograph me. I agreed, and sometime later six artful prints arrived in the mail. They were since disbursed among friends who asked for them one by one, until now only one is left.

I slipped back into my parents' home later that day, with no one the wiser (or so I thought) as I got into the shower. In the old days it would have been, "Just wait until your father gets home." That invariably meant you'd be running for your bed to pull the covers up over you so he'd leave no marks when he pulled off his belt and gave you the strap, but not this time. It was actually a few nights later. When he arrived home, Mother called me out from my room, and they asked me to come with them on a drive. They wanted to talk to me.

My father parked at a strip mall near the house. The sun was just setting and the streetlights began to come on. Mother turned around in the front passenger seat and told me, "We know you weren't at Linda's the other night. We called." Interesting, Linda hadn't called to warn me. I was mortified. I could not tell them the truth. I could not take the chance that they might put me away. So in silence, I suffered listening to my father's lecture on sex. He didn't look directly at me, though he checked the rearview mirror twice to be sure I was still listening. He said it wasn't as if there was something wrong with sex "itself" but that within the act of lovemaking there was an entwining of souls that should be saved for "your husband". I would only understand what he meant sometime later. I was after all still a virgin.

I was surprised that they didn't venture further and ask for details of my whereabouts. Obviously, they thought that I'd been having sex, but perhaps they were afraid of freaking me out. Clearly, they were deeply concerned.

My body was blossoming to perfection, when I started starving myself. I was tall enough to easily appear slender, my shoulders were broad, my arms beautifully shaped, with peasant hands. On my small torso hung alabaster blue-veined globes with pink nipples. A tiny waist with boxy hips, atop long slender legs, standing on pretty feet! My face I thought plain, but my body was that of a beautiful woman. I pulled at my skin, and if I could lift it off the bone, I was still not thin enough. Funny how I thought of it, "thin enough". My biggest meal of the day was a large slice of chocolate cake with a thick layer of fudge frosting and a carton of milk at around noon then hardly anything else. At dinner with my parents, I would pick at the pot roast, eat one pea and a bit of mashed potatoes. Then I'd push the plate away. Mother's eyes teared up, and Father pretended not to notice.

When I asked for a psychologist, he said, "Forget it!" I shook my head wearily and went to bed. Moments later they both came into my room and sat on either side of my bed.

My father regarded me deeply then and asked, "Are you unhappy?"

"Yes," I said softly.

"Why?" he asked helplessly. I was too exhausted to explain the anxiety I couldn't shake. He finally agreed to let me see someone. Problem is that when I did meet with a psychologist, I dismissed her after the second visit. I said it was because she had not read Camus and was therefore not educated enough to help me. The real reason was because she asked for information that I was not prepared to give her.

My friend Lori was the vamp of all vamps. Her mother Jane was one of my dearest friends. When I met Jane, she was dying of emphysema. She was intelligent, kind, and had done seven years of Jungian therapy. I guess I imagined that made her some kind of an authority.

"You're going to die," she said. "Do you hear me? If you don't stop, you'll die."

She took several deep breaths in exasperation and blurted out with some effort, "You're anorexic! It's called anorexia!" I've always appreciated friends who are unafraid of telling me the truth.

"I've got news for you," she said, "the emaciated look is not pretty." Honestly, I was deeply pleased by my thinness and would like to have been thinner. Jane asked, "Why shouldn't you be nurtured?"

I didn't know the answer, though I began to wonder if it was somehow related to the fact that as a child (of perfect health) my most constant vision in daydreams was getting sick, going to the hospital, and being laid up. Mother never failed to play her motherly role when we, as children, were ill. Even now the theme often recurs in my daydreams: I take deathly ill, am taken from my sickbed by the love of my life, and live happily ever after, almost as if sickness is a pre-requisite to being loved. Most regrettable of all is that this diet put me at the mercy of my own merciless ego. I was 17-years-old, 5'8" and weighed 96 pounds. I hadn't had a period in nine months, and I wasn't expecting a virgin birth. Something was wrong.

Once again there seemed to be an intervention of a higher sort. I woke one morning with a start, leapt out of bed, jumped into my jeans, and headed off to school in a great rush. Without a single thought, I went straight to the research library. I walked directly over to the psychology stacks as if in a trance. I reached for a book on the shelf before me, Alfred Adler's Understanding Human Nature. I opened it to an arbitrary page, a chapter titled "The Seventeen-Year-Old Starvation Diet." There it was written: "This hunger strike is considered a wish to reject the feminine role by stunting the feminine development. It is also seen as an attempt to control those around you like a father, a man."

As soon as I realized it was some sort of neurosis, I stopped. I remember my father always using the word "neurotic" with great disdain. I saw it as weakness. I built a character, a strong one. People would take exception to it all my life, but it would serve me well. I would soon find a new way to control myself and my surroundings.

*

It was the dawning of the sexual revolution. Birth control was widely accepted, and the arguments about abortion were raging. Women's Liberation declared women and men to be absolutely equal. Some might ask, "Why lower ourselves?" and "Does equal mean the same?" Women were to have the same freedom as men, sexually speaking.

Why not have as many lovers as one wished without consideration or awareness of any consequences whatsoever? For me, the thought of marrying someone and then finding out that they were not a good lover would be a tragedy not worth risking. And as Camus said, "Why should it be necessary to love rarely in order to love well?" Exactly!

I wandered into a new shop on my way to the laundry near my parent's home in Covina, Ca. Dropping my bag on the floor, I asked out loud, "Where am I? What is this place?"

The walls were covered with pegboards and hooks. A few of the guitars were already hanging. From one of the practice rooms in the back sauntered Adonis, as I live and breathe! Tall, slender, and elegant even in his jeans, wearing a fitted pale blue t-shirt. His black hair was cut to show off his soft curls. His face was perfectly carved. Thick dramatic lashes framed his dark brown eyes. He paused a moment regarding me over his wire-rimmed glasses, reminiscent of those recently made popular by Lennon. Then smiling broadly, his thick lips parting to reveal his perfect white teeth, he strode across the room and stretched out his hand enthusiastically.

"This is The Guitar Shop, and my name is T.B."

I was attracted to him immediately. When he sat down to play the guitar for me with his long slender fingers and nails picking at the strings, I knew I had to have him. But he was twenty-eight, and I was jailbait. Still, I would pursue him relentlessly.

We spoke for a while between songs. I lied and told him I was attending MSAC, the local Junior College. He played something I knew, and I began to sing. He was surprised and pleased. He saw in me a new singing partner perhaps.

He walked me out as I left, touching me gently as though we were already lovers. I would see him again and again. I bought a guitar and began taking lessons from one of his partners, Bert.

T.B. asked me to sing at the Blue Grass concerts with him. Of course, I said yes. It meant spending long hours practicing the songs together. Perfect! Sometimes he would sit on the stool behind the counter staring at me while he dragged his tongue across his teeth, like a wolf, licking his chops.

The partners, Bert, and especially the schoolteacher, Spencer, were increasingly concerned about our relationship. By then I'd confessed I was only seventeen. T.B. had told me about a young dark-haired woman he'd sung with before, something about their relationship being a cry for help from each of them. What he didn't mention was that she was also seventeen. Her parents caught on and had him arrested. The judge told him next time he'd throw the book at him. I wouldn't hear about this until I was eighteen and having a brief, though wonderful, affair with Bert. He was an excellent lover, the first and only one to inform me that most women have feeling in their breasts, that there was a direct connection between the breasts and the clitoris. Good that he told me. I pretended henceforth.

Bert was driving and Spence was in the passenger seat one night on our way back from a Hootenanny. T.B. easily coaxed me into the back of the station wagon, where there happened to be a mattress. It got hot and heavy quickly, and Spence went crazy. He demanded that we return to our backseats, something about losing the shop and their licenses. There it was, we were out in the open. T.B. asked if

I'd like to go with him to see Hendrix. A real date! I was thrilled. No problem. I could go to a concert.

It was April 25th, 1970. We met at the shop and went to see Jimmy Hendrix at the Forum. I was privileged to hear him play "The Star Spangled Banner". Magnificent does not describe it! That would turn out to be the high point of the evening for me. T.B. turned to me halfway through the concert and asked if I'd like to leave. And be alone with him? Of course! So we wound up at his place, which turned out to be above the garage at his parents' home.

His bed was like a cubbyhole. He invited me to lay down. Soon, my long green corduroy skirt was around my waist. He rolled on top of me, came inside of me, and rolled off of me. He stood up quickly, wanting to get me out of there, and told me, "It isn't like you weren't expecting this."

I was speechless. There was no blood. Turns out I have what's called an "elastic" hymen—ever tight. He took me back to the shop. I walked home, almost feeling sorry for him.

Not long after, the vamp Lori found her way to his shop. It took her all of fifteen minutes to get T.B. to kiss her and even less time to come and tell me about it. It may have been the timing or just the thought that he would kiss her so casually after just "doing" me, but it was over. Besides, I was certain he would never improve as a lover.

Several years later I hunted him down in Redondo Beach. He was surprised when he opened his apartment door and found me standing there. I don't know exactly what I was looking for, contrition perhaps. There was none. He claimed he was sorry he couldn't change who he was and pointed out that my life was seemingly going well for me. He was right. I wanted to blame and punish him for something I had clearly created myself. Ah well, I wrote this sometime later to his partner Bert.

When the land lies fallow for the season
When the door closes
As we, lying together, to each other
And my love is flung at your back
Embrace the sweet relief
Bow down in the field empty with you
Are free

Chapter Three — Grot

I was awakened by a slight rap at the door, opened just enough for Jean's hand to appear, laden with grapes, posed as an offering for me to see. I was delighted, leaping out of bed to greet him with a big hug. I wanted to pull him back onto the sheets with me but he had other ideas.

"Come on, get dressed. We're going on a picnic."

I jumped into my jeans, pulled on a soft pretty sweater, and we were off. First, we went to the boucherie for a few slices of meat and a bottle of wine. Then we went to the fromagerie for cheese, to the boulangerie for a baguette, and lastly to the confectionneur for the best dark chocolate truffles I would ever eat. He knew my passion for chocolate. How sweet it is when boys plan a date so carefully!

Picnic in hand, we entered the beautiful park called Bois de Boulogne. It was my first time there. We strolled hand in hand as lovers do. Everywhere there were others whom we seemed to resemble, as if engaged or about to be. Young families with dear little children in a world we could easily have been a part of, were it not for the fact that I was headed in another direction entirely. Something in me longed for the life I saw around me but I could not settle for it. I was driven from within to find something else, and deep inside, Jean knew it. Still, for this lovely day, we would pretend that it would always be like this, wrapped in the timeless air of Love.

Two years before, I was introduced to Grotowski's book, *Towards a Poor Theater*. I read it and devoured it. Grot's call to the "holy actor" appealed to my quest for purity. He said, "We do not teach people to pretend, because we pretend in daily life."

I was already aware of the mask, the play, and the pretense. I wanted the truth about myself, my existence. I had always had a powerful sense of something pervading from within that was hidden from me, something essential to my understanding of this life that I desperately needed and could hardly bear to live without. I prayed ceaselessly as a child for it to be revealed to me. Then the prayer became an angry demand of a God perhaps deaf.

I knew I could act, but I was not interested in selling myself to Hollywood. I was willing to give myself totally to the search, determined to succeed or die trying. Grotowski's work offered an opportunity for self-discovery or as he would say, "a meeting with the self". I put all else aside to prepare for the chance to work with him.

I found a brilliant teacher locally who knew Grot personally and was using many of his exercises and techniques to train a small group of brave actors. His name was Leonidas Dudarew-Ossetynski. I called him "O". He was a Lithuanian prince by birth, stripped of his royalty by the Communist occupation of Eastern Europe. He had been an actor in Warsaw before WWII, along with his friend, Karol Wojtyla, who later became Pope John Paul II. During the war, O was put in a prison camp for helping Jews out of the Warsaw ghetto.

Many people have told me that during the war there were no Catholics and no Jews, only Poles. Strangely, O said that those who had been misers before internment in the camp became the most generous, and those who had been the most giving before became greedy.

When we first met, each of us stretched out our arms to shake hands and took a step back at the same time. The overwhelming sensation of meeting someone I already knew made that the most unusual introduction of my life.

I had stumbled across the concept of reincarnation somewhere along the way. Without believing in it, I used it as one would a fairy tale to explain strange feelings I could not otherwise understand like déjà vu.

Once I had a dream about living in a camp. I stood with nine other men around an immense hole. We were digging another mass grave. As a protest we each slammed our shovels into the ground and refused to go on digging. Despite the insistent threats of the many SS Guards surrounding us, we stood steadfast in our decision. We were ordered to line up along a plank that stretched out into a channel of filthy water, lined by high berms. I was last in line and so first to feel the cold German Luger at my right temple. I don't remember hearing the sound of the gun going off. Everything just went black. Then I saw myself in this life telephoning my mother to tell her, "Oh, Mother, it's wonderful! I was just killed in Auschwitz, and here I am again!"

Many years later in Jerusalem, I went to pay my respects at Yad Vashem, Israel's official memorial to the victims of the Holocaust. I have never been able to look at pictures or artifacts from that time: the gold fillings, the hair, the shoes, the clothing; and the sight of a Swastika always turns me white as a ghost.

So I went through the museum with my eyes closed, until I came upon a room filled with scale models of all the camps. I walked directly over to look at one in particular, and there it was: the barracks, the berm'd channels, and the planks laid across them. It was Auschwitz! Eventually I surmised that perhaps O and I had known each other before as actors in Warsaw and, strangely enough, that would mean he had known me twice in one lifetime as two entirely different people!

I studied with O in preparation to go on to Grotowski. There were not usually more than six students in his studio at a time in a small barren workroom located directly above the budding improv group known as the Groundlings. We met three consecutive days a week: Friday night, Saturday night, and Sunday mornings, each five-hour sessions. There were no breaks. Class began with warm-up exercises that appeared simple enough, made arduous by their intent to break down our resistances. Walking forward in a circle, while grabbing onto our ankles, then the same position walking backwards, sideways, right, and left. Then it was repeated grasping the toes. Then all the same over again but with the legs crossed. It always made me feel as if I was in chains.

The class was never easy. Whatever exercise was mastered was either dropped or the difficulty level increased. Many were designed to bring forth a quaking of the body as well as the emotions. The physical pain that was involved in so much of the work was to be tolerated. It seemed the more you resisted the pain the greater it became. Still, there was enjoyment and even fun to be found in the amazing growth and discoveries within the work.

At times, it seemed we were being trained to become the Uberman. There was the Flying Tiger exercise where we would "fly" horizontally over the backs of one, two, three, or four of the actors, braced on their hands and knees across the hard linoleum floor. Then there were the Ancient Chinese Resonator techniques for the voice, which I delighted and excelled in so much that I later taught them.

A young Bier Russian, Yarosha, helped O by demonstrating some of the exercises and teaching Tai Chi, Kathakali, Dynamic Hatha Yoga, Balinese dance, as well as No and Kabuki theater. The extensive training helped turn me into someone who could do extraordinary things.

Ossetynski thought he recognized some profound talent in me and perhaps pinned his hopes of regaining fame on the outcome of my career. The pressure on me was great, and the frustration for him perhaps even greater. He told me he would help me on three conditions: "First lower your voice by one octave. Second, change the way you walk. And third, change your personality."

I did lower my voice by an octave.

Meanwhile, Yarosha fell in love with me, and we soon became lovers. He was a Sikh. He told me he had heard a music within himself that made Beethoven boring. I, in the arrogance of my youth, took exception to this, unable to imagine what he was talking about. I had loved Beethoven since I was a child and was inspired by his music to live my life with the same intense passion I felt in his compositions. When Yarosha asked me to marry him, I ended the affair.

The last hour of each class was devoted to the study of Chi Gung. I realize now there was good reason to leave that

47

until the end. After four hours of exhausting work, our resistance was so low that it actually increased the possibility of grasping this ancient technique for routing energy. I felt for years that I would never accomplish it. My mind fought fiercely against what it could neither perceive nor understand. O would instruct us in his deep voice and heavy Polish accent.

"Stand with your feet shoulder width apart. Don't lock the knees. Now, imagine in the palm of your hand is a flashlight. Then let that light flash upon the front wall."

I assumed the position and tried over and over again. Session after session, week after week, year after year, nothing—until the day when it came streaming forth in rays of light from the palms of my hands.

I would soon learn I could control both the color and the intensity of that light. Ultimately the energy itself seemed to be instructing me from within, and I would discover to my complete surprise, that I could use it to heal others. Though I had yet to develop the compassion needed to want to help others, the power itself forced me to utilize it!

*

Beneath the net of leaves woven upon the branches above us, sprawled across our picnic spread, Jean expressed his love, "Je t'aime."

"Je t'aime aussi," I replied.

I enjoyed every moment of that day, so full of tenderness. In the night we wrapped around our passion. Then in the morning, sitting on the edge of my bed, somehow Jean realized that I thought the verb aimer meant "to like" not "to love".

"So which is it?" he demanded to know.

I hesitated just a second and felt his heart sink. "Of course, I love you, I really do!" I worked on him believing me.

It rained for several days. With the clouds still dense in the sky as evening drew near, I found my way to the Palais de Justice. I was among the first to arrive at the immense iron gates that led to the entrance of La Sainte Chapelle where Grotowski's actors were about to perform their current work, *Apocalypsis cum Figuris*.

Standing near me, also waiting intently, were two women whose personas attracted me. We were all dressed in black, the uniforms of our serious natures. Our link was so obvious, we recognized one another immediately, shaking hands and sharing our intent to join Grotowski in his work. Emmanuelle and Chloe had been friends since they were teenagers. Still it seemed I had arrived on cue, and the friendship that grew between us was clearly destiny.

In the damp chilly air we watched and waited at the gate for Grotowski to arrive and handpick his audience from the gathering. Only those whom he chose would be let in.

When he appeared and began the selection, I was the first to be chosen. My new friends quickly followed. We all stood in the downstairs hall before being led up the winding stone staircase to Sainte Chapelle's upper sanctuary, where the ceiling arches are vaulted 150 feet. We sat on the floor against the walls, hushed and hungry for the performance about to begin.

I cannot do justice with words to describe what I experienced. I will never forget when the actor playing Jon tore open a loaf of French country bread, reached into it, tore out the soft core, and hurled it like a baseball at the body of the Innocent. It struck him with a thud like a rock. Ryszard Cieslak, Grot's lead actor, played the role of the Innocent.

At one point, Ryszard was crouched in child's pose on the floor. He cried out in anguish but his voice came not from his body. It came from the top of the ceiling and floated down like a leaf gracefully falling. When the performance was finished, the audience was too stunned to clap and remained as if frozen in their places for several minutes before almost reluctantly ambling up to leave. I was still unable or unwilling to move, longing to absorb and retain every moment of the experience.

Finally, one of Grot's people helped me up. They led me back down the spiral staircase to the grand hall below. I was asked to leave a number where I could be reached. I wrote down Madame's, as there was no other, and put "dans la matinée" ("in the afternoon") because it was mostly the only time I was there.

Grotowski himself took the paper from my hand and looked at me a little strangely. "Dans la matinée, oui?" he asked.

"Yes," I replied rather shyly and foolishly not explaining the time restriction.

On my way home I felt every step of my feet upon the ground. I was enlivened and inspired as never before. Anything and everything was possible! I was determined to continue my goal of joining Grotowski with renewed resolution.

More than a week went by, and still no call from Grotowski.

"Suppose he doesn't call at all, now that I am useless to anyone else?" I wondered, as I walked through the streets.

I waited until I was sure he had left Paris, then strangely a little relieved, my hands unclenched. What I did not know at the time was, had I been chosen to go make "Holiday" with them in the south of France, it would have meant the end of my chance to join the encounter at the Theatre Lab in January. Further, I would later learn that those participants were buried alive with only straws to breathe through and left there for several hours until they were dug up for the resurrection celebration. My severe claustrophobia would have made that impossible.

Meanwhile, I got word from Pamela Zarubica also known as "Suzy Cream Cheese" (made famous by Frank Zappa), that she was coming down from London to Paris to see me and visit the grave of her dear friend Jim Morrison. She was living in Chelsea at the home of Toni Howard, the manager of T-Rex.

It couldn't have been worse timing for me, but I couldn't say no. There was no one quite like her. I had met her in the Rainbow Bar and Grill on Sunset Strip the year before, when she came tumbling down the stairs from the private club, smashed on Quaaludes. I offered to get her some coffee thinking she was drunk.

She said snarling, "Coffee? That stuff is poison!" She settled for tea at the bar, and our friendship began.

Pam was a publicist for Playboy Records. Her business cards read "Ms. Information". She was beautiful and brash with long, straight, dark brown hair that she was constantly running her fingers through. Her nails were always painted jade green to match the jade rings she wore on each of her fingers.

Pam's speech was sometimes slurred, likely caused by her excessive use of tranquilizers. Still, she had an extraordinarily vivacious personality that drew other extraordinary people to her like a magnet. I was intrigued. Knowing her landed me straight into the middle of the music industry. It was amusing to think I could have shown myself as a singer at that time but chose not to.

Jim Morrison slept on her floor just before his first concert at the Roxy when the Doors opened the path to fame for him. Frank Zappa referred to her as his Suzy Cream Cheese. Later she wrote an autobiography titled "The Cheese Stands Alone." How true it was. So no, I could not bring myself to tell her she could not come to visit me in Paris.

Pam stayed with me in my small servant's room. She was there only a few days when, returning from visiting Morrison's grave, she was struck by a car. She spent the next month laid up in the American Hospital at Neuilly in a brace due to a hairline crack in her cervical vertebrae. It was an hour Metro ride from my place and coincidentally, the area where Jean's father lived.

Now my time was divided between work, Jean, and the hospital. I was still waiting to hear from the Theatre Lab to learn whether I would be accepted to join what Grot called the "Rencontre Preliminaire" ("Preliminary Meeting").

When Thanksgiving arrived, Jean and I went to a boucherie, picked up a cold pheasant and everything else I could think of for the feast and headed out to visit Pam. I remember how grateful she was. Afterwards Jean took me to his father's place. It was a beautiful upscale home in Neuilly. His father had once been the chess champion of Europe. Jean was proud of him, and I was proud of Jean.

He was determined to be his own man, accountable to himself alone. I understood this, as I too valued my independence.

The time came for Pam to leave the hospital and return to London. Toni came to get her and checked into the Paris Hilton. I went there to say goodbye. We talked a while. Pam said she wanted me to remember two important pieces of advice. "First: all you ever need to remember, no matter how drunk or stoned you may get, is your name and the Hilton Hotel. Because you can always ask any cab driver to take you to the Hilton and as long as you know your name, they will check you in and deal with the money in the morning." I have not tested that one out.

"And further, I've known people who died because they didn't know when to leave." Toni brought out a hash pipe and we each took a hit. Unfortunately, I stood up too quickly and blacked out immediately, hitting the Formica coffee table on my way down.

I had blacked out many times before in my life. The first time I was ten years old at a Halloween party. Everything went dark inside except a rim of light silhouetting my body, and then I was on the floor as if my skeleton had broken into a bag of bones. It was embarrassing being helped up off the floor by the other children. Worse, it was at the house of a boy I had a crush on. I walked home soon after. Never told my parents. And never gave that boy another thought.

When I regained consciousness, my face was bleeding. I asked for a mirror. Pam refused to give me one, pleading with me not to look, while Toni called the front desk. I got up and went to the window where I could see my reflection in the glass against the night sky. My face was hanging open in a crescent cut at the right cheekbone. My despair was so deep I was beyond weeping. How could I go to Grotowski's Theatre looking like this? I was taken by ambulance back to the American Hospital's emergency room, where I was gratefully sewn up by a plastic surgeon, who just happened to be on shift that night.

Then it was time to say goodbye to Pamela. Sadly, unbeknownst to me, it was the last time I would ever see her. I loved her and I miss her. I was the recipient of so much sweetness from friends and lovers at that time in my life. Yet secretly, I felt guilty that I wasn't capable of quite returning it. It would be decades before I realized I had loved them all.

It was noon before I arrived at Madame's front door, four hours late for work. I dared to take the resident's elevator because I was still feeling quite injured. As soon as Madame saw my face, she dropped her fury and concern over my tardiness and went into motherly nurse mode. I guess at last I felt free to weep.

"What will people think?" I asked her strangely. "I look like I've been in a knife fight."

Madame did not yet know I would likely be leaving soon for Poland. "Just tell them, 'La tête m'a tourné et je suis tombée par terre' ('My head turned and I fell to the ground'). It could happen to anyone!" she added with bolstering confidence. Bizarrely enough, not long after the stiches were taken out, I began to experience severe headaches pounding up the right side of my head. I wished it had something to do with the fall, but I knew it did not.

*

When I was 19, I had lived in a beautiful Spanish-style apartment in Westwood Village that I'd taken over from my friend Eleanor when she left for Paris. One day while working on extreme facial exercises intended to create masks, something strange happened. Suddenly, the right side of my face was paralyzed. Whatever movement I made on the left side was completely distorted. It was ghastly, almost monstrous.

My doctor told me it was called Bell's palsy, a virus attacking the facial nerve, causing it to swell and impairing its ability to pass impulses through the tiny bone structure behind the ear, thus freezing the face on that side. Dr. Salik said it would probably go away by itself and that there was nothing else he could do for me. His suggestion that it would go away was the most useful message he could have offered me. Just as strangely as it had appeared, it did disappear after nineteen days.

Unfortunately, a year later I began to experience severe pain behind my ear on that same side. Again my face shut down! I went to the ENT Department at UCLA and was quickly told that if it was the second time I had it, most likely it would not go away by itself. The doctor suggested surgery to drill around the nerve where it passed through the inner ear.

"What are my chances if I allow you to do that?" I asked.

"50/50," he responded. "Fifty percent chance I can cure you, fifty percent chance you'll be deformed for life."

"Did you hear me say I'm a theatre student?" I asked incredulously.

"I am sorry," he said without emotion and then excused

himself momentarily from the room. He had given me several sheets of paper for the tests he planned on administering. I tore them into tiny pieces until he returned. Then I stood up, threw them in his face like confetti, and walked out the door without another word.

Ossetynski and Yarosha had been trying to convince me to see Dr. Sigfreid Kanauel, a 92-year-old MD and homeopathic physician from Moscow University. I was reluctant, not a fan of alternative medicine. But, as I walked away from UCLA, I was willing to try anything. I was told that Dr. Kanauel's patients came from around the world to see him. When I first entered his examining room, I was surprised to find the walls covered with raw wood shelves filled with thousands of homeopathic tincture bottles.

As I laid down on his examining table, the first thing I noticed about Dr. Kanauel was that he appeared much younger than he actually was. He was dignified and possessed an air of steadied confidence. I failed to notice the depth of his kindness as he approached me. He took out a large lightbulb attached to a box and held it near my face. I closed my eyes and began to weep out of the only eye that could still cry.

"What am I doing here with this quack?" I thought to myself silently as Kanauel continued his examination.

"Can you help me?" I asked pitifully.

"Yes," he said assuredly.

I began to feel a wave of healing love emanating from him as he went from bottle to bottle, filling up a syringe to give me injections in places I'd never had them before, this organ, then that limb. He gave me a small bottle of tincture and told me to take ten drops, three times a day and come back in four days. Though he charged his patients $25 a visit, he treated me for free. In exchange, I brought him flowers and homemade cakes. In two months, I had my face back.

I saw Kanauel as a doctor and a saint. I thought that doctors should be called to their vocations like priests. He had cured more with the depth of his humanity than with the brilliance of his medical prowess.

I asked him on my way out, "Will it ever return?"

He replied, "Nothing is forever, not even death."

*

So there I was with a deep purple scar upon my too-white cheek, and the excruciating pain was again pounding up my head. Fortunately, Eleanor knew of the leading acupuncturist in all Europe. Interestingly enough, he was also a 92-year-old, but Chinese and living in St. Germain des Prés.

It was a little difficult finding his place, tucked away in the 6eme district. I finally found it on the top floor of a beautiful old building. He greeted me at the door and instructed me to go lay down on a green velvet tufted-back chaise lounge that you might have expected to find in Freud's office.

"Should I remove my clothes?"

He shook his head and began sinking needles into me. To my surprise, with rare exception, there was no pain. There was a sound as the needles were tapped in, that of a pin going into a pincushion. He put a hundred needles in me, most around my right eye, mouth, face, head, and neck. The rest he placed masterfully straight through my clothes! Though I have had many acupuncture treatments since from world-renowned doctors, I have never again found anyone who could put needles through clothes!

When finished with the placements, he turned down the lights and instructed me to rest there a while. I dared not move. There was a strange sensation as if I was floating, like a cloud just above my body. After 45 minutes he returned and began removing the needles. When I stood up, I realized the pain had vanished. I paid him, fumbling and unable to sufficiently express my profound gratitude, try though I did. He had saved me. For the time being I could go forward.

The following morning, as I sat eating my petit dejeuner, Madame entered the kitchen holding a light green envelope, already opened. She appeared all at once angry and hurt. She spoke before handing it to me. "This telegram arrived for you late yesterday afternoon. I opened it thinking it might be some terrible news that I would have to find a way to break gently to you. I am very disappointed to find that you've been secretly planning to leave here very soon." With that she handed me the envelope and walked out of the kitchen without another word.

I read the telegram and leapt for joy, barely able to keep myself from yelping. I had been accepted at the Theatre Laboratory to attend the "Rencontre Preliminaire"! I would have to leave for Wrocław, Poland, in a few weeks. When I told Jean, he was happy for me though not really surprised.

Jean took me to the train at Gard de Nord. He stayed with me on the platform as we waited until it was time for me to board the Nord Orient Express bound for Poland and beyond. I tried to assure him that I would return and then we would be together. He clicked his tongue against the roof of his mouth and gently shook his head. "No, it cannot be."

"Mais pourquoi?" ("But why?") I entreated.

"Because we are from different cultures. It will never work."

"C'est pas vrai." ("That is not true.")

"Mais oui, c'est vrai." ("But yes, it is true.") His whole body rocked softly side to side in despair. Funny how we make up explanations to protect ourselves from the truth, which in this case was though we would be together again, I was on the road to myself alone.

We embraced and kissed. My love and desire for him was the only thing that made it difficult to leave. As the tears began to stream down my cheeks, he looked deep into my eyes and said, "Try to be discreet." Then I was off.

The train pulled away from the station. I rested my head against the window and let myself fall into the hypnotic scenes of country landscapes quickly passing by. I confess a widened sense of freedom came over me. I was on my way to catch my destiny, uncertain what awaited me. Grot had said that it wasn't a question of success or failure but that one might "miss a meeting with oneself."

I had been careful to choose an empty cabin. I rigged a rope tying one end to my wrist and the other to the handle of the sliding door so that I could stretch out on the bench and sleep. If someone tried to open the door, it would pull me off the bench.

The train stopped at four separate stations in Berlin. I was uncomfortable being in Germany. As we rolled through the Black Forest, I saw only darkness and blood. When we reached the border of Poland, a large guard slammed open my cabin door and ordered in a deep voice, "Passportah!" As if I would resist showing it to him.

We stopped at the small town of Poznan, where my ancestors had come from. Then onward, plowing through the falling snow, across Poland to Warsaw. I would be spending Vegilia, Christmas Eve, at the home of O's mother-in-law and his step-daughters.

O was on his ninth and last marriage at that time. I was told he had stood knee-deep in snow beneath Pani Anna Romanska's window, screaming for her to come down to him or he would stay there until he died. In the morning, Anna found him lying half-frozen in the snow. She helped him up, brushed him off, and married him. Anna was a kind and elegant woman with aristocratic manners. He was an inveterate womanizer. After years of a seemingly successful marriage, he broke it by having an affair with the 17-year-old daughter of a very famous Russian actor. That was sometime after my six years of study with him.

When I arrived in Warsaw, I was driven around the city in circles several times by a cab driver, who realized I was a stranger and so inept at Polish I couldn't even properly dress him down.

Many, many złotys (coins) later, I arrived at the Romanskas. They were very kind and ingratiating to me. The grandmother and Anna's two daughters lived in a small apartment consisting of two rooms, a small kitchen, and a bathroom. This was common throughout postwar Poland. The front room doubled as a salon and bedroom for the grandmother. The two sisters, Katya and Maya, shared the other room.

Katya spoke several languages including English, Russian, German, and Chinese. Maya smoked twice as many cigarettes as I did and seemed quite nervous, her eyes constantly darting around as if she was searching for something to comfort her. Unfortunately, her English was no better than my Polish. They shared with me what little they had. Katya stayed in Grandma's room and I with Maya in the other.

I went down in the morning to buy us some bread at the nearby store. The loaves were set unwrapped on the shelves with a tiny piece of paper stuck into them, which I presumed was some sort of Communist slogan. Still, it was delicious!

Russian soldiers marched everywhere four-by-four deep. In Poland, after the cold, one noticed the silence. You could actually hear the mood music being played in the department store. Professors and other intellectuals dared only to whisper even in their own homes!

I inquired as to what happened to them during WWII, realizing that all of old Warsaw had been rebuilt with the help of Russian money, down to the cracks in the walls, an exact replica as if the city was itself a museum!

I was told they picked up rocks and bottles in the streets to throw at the invading Nazis in determined attempts to drive them back. Because of this, Hitler threatened to level Warsaw to the ground. And he did. There was nothing but chimneys left standing. Women told me not only could they not find their homes after the bombing; they could not even find the streets they lived on!

I must say it did not help my general disdain for Paris. I used to think, "Paris is beautiful, but it is not my beauty." I was in my youth still unable to forgive them for turning over their Jewish neighbors rather than see their monuments fall.

Upon my return to Paris I would declare brutally, "Après Varsovie, on ne peut voir Paris, que comme une femme qui ouvre les jambes devant Hitler," which means, "After Warsaw, one cannot view Paris as more than the woman who opened her legs to Hitler." It would take age, wisdom, and compassion to get over that.

On Christmas Eve morning, I woke to find a carp swimming in the bathtub! Grandma was preparing the Christmas dinner. The carp would soon be killed and stewed with fruit. Where she found the money to do anything, I'll never know. Probably Anna was sending money from the States whenever she could. The punishment for trading money on the black market was death. Still Grandma was able to trade me 90 złotys for every dollar I had. Since the average salary was 50 złotys a month, I suddenly found myself rich.

Christmas came and went.

I left a few days later I left for Wrocław by train. I will always be grateful to the Romanskas for offering me shelter while I saw Warsaw.

Chapter Four — Wiesław

The train rolled through Krakow. I thought of the newspaper reporter from the Russian-controlled Pravda, who had dogged me through Warsaw, no doubt under Ossetynski's orders. He had asked if I'd like a tour of Auschwitz, just outside Krakow. I told him "no" emphatically. I believed I couldn't go there and still make it to Wrocław. I don't know if the train passed by the camp or if I merely fell asleep. Perhaps it diverged. I don't recall seeing it in the distance, as I looked forward to Wrocław and awakened there.

I was sent to live with friends of O. The family lived in a luxury townhouse, four flights up a wide mahogany staircase. I was given a room with a yellow tile furnace taking up one corner of the room and pale-yellow walls. It was especially kind of them to let me stay, even if only as a favor to Ossetynski.

The first time I went out alone for dinner, I discovered I couldn't read the menu. The Communists had failed to translate it for me! I wound up having to go into the kitchen and point to the food I wanted to eat. I felt all at once grateful and illiterate. The meal was absolutely delicious, including the cabbage with tomato, potato, and fish. I was touched by their kindness and willingness to improvise for the sake of communicating and getting me fed!

The next day I bounded down the stairs to the street and stepped into a bakery for a lovely apple tart. I ate it while I stood at the Taxi sign and waited my turn for a cab. I was headed to the town center where the Theatre Laboratorium was located, just next door to the famous town clock.

Emmanuelle and Chloe had also arrived. We found each other in the "milk bar" searching for something to eat. Milk, yogurt, and borscht were all available there. I had the soup and sat with my friends. We were all electric with excitement, on the border of our dreams. Emmanuelle was quiet in the background, ever observing and taking notes.

Chloe and I went on cold walks through the snow, marching aimlessly over the icy streets as the frigid air flushed our cheeks.

Chloe declared as if joking, "I am a broken woman!"

"I am a completely broken woman," I retorted.

"Exactement!" she affirmed.

"Absolument!" I added.

"I am only 20 years old and I have already been with three men. And the last one "m'a frappée sur la tête avec sa chaussure" ("hit me on the head with his shoe"), she said, still in disbelief. She was quite animated as she described the attack.

"Do you believe? I let him hit me with his shoe!"

"Mais, c'est pas vrai!" I feigned disbelief.

"Mais oui, c'est vrai. I am a completely broken woman!"

"Moi aussi, I am a broken woman, absolument!" I attested loudly.

"Exactement!" We would both periodically burst out laughing.

"Et toi, tu en as eu combien?" ("And you, how many did you have?") Chloe asked innocently.

I paused for a moment considering and then just told her the truth, "Vingt-cinq" ("Twenty-five.").

"Vingt-cinq?" she repeated in disbelief.

I raised my eyebrows, and nodded my head shamelessly.

"Mais tu es vraiment une pécheresse!" ("But you are truly a sinning woman!") she declared without a hint of judgment. And again we laughed. I wasn't aware that twenty-five lovers was an extraordinary number for a woman of twenty-one years.

*

Soon after I left T.B., I met George at a party. He was handsome, very manly and kind. He lived in a quaint old home that had been built at the end of the 19th century, beautifully trimmed with mahogany moldings and a lovely stained-glass window with a portrait of two sisters above the mantel.

His two roommates were both graduate students at a prestigious film school in L.A., where George was director of the RNT division, making nurse's training films. As my only experience with actual sexual intercourse had been that of a log rolling over me, George was more than happy to teach me. I was absolutely aghast when he went down on me and even more so when he presented his popsicle to me. Still I was responsive, eager and willing to please. I quickly got the picture that I was in an animal form, the human animal. I would come to appreciate the wild beast in me, though it would be tempered by humanity.

I lived with him only briefly. On my 18th birthday, George took me to San Francisco to spend the weekend as guests in the townhouse of his friends, a married couple, both with PhDs in Psychology. That night the husband placed stereo headphones on me and blasted Janis Joplin in my ears. I had never heard her before. My life changed in flash.

Next morning, as George and I leaned out their front window staring down at the street, I blurted out under my breath, "I hate you." He did not deserve that, had done nothing to deserve that. I suppose I felt trapped, living together. I was terrified of being held back against the destiny I felt marching beside me.

A week later he came home from work to find all my things gone and me with them. Then I refused to answer the phone at the girl's boarding house near Cal State where I had gone. When I finally agreed to see him, it was only for a moment to say goodbye. I am sorry for that.

Shortly after signing up for a semester of classes at Cal State, I ran into Lorin on the second-floor library bridge. He was my sister Kate's first love. They met at Bishop Amat High School when they were in A Man for All Seasons together. Lorin played Thomas Moore well, and Kate played his daughter. She was as beautiful and brilliant on stage as everywhere else. He fell in love with her and I am sure loves her still.

Perhaps she too was terrified of love. She had broken up with him some years before and was on her first marriage at the time. Lorin was a brilliant jazz poet. Kate was the subject of many of his poems and I of even more. Not because he loved me more but merely because he found me a more interesting subject. The content was not always flattering. Sadly, he was never widely published, much to the literary world's loss.

He was exceedingly soft-spoken, often to the point of being inaudible. He would teach me all I knew about the jazz artists of our time as he allowed me to thumb through his collections of Miles Davis, Thelonious Monk, and John Coltrane as if their records were made of precious gold. Coltrane was my favorite, especially "A Love Supreme".

I respected Lorin's intelligence, his gentle nature, and his humanity. He was wonderfully passionate. He knew how to make fire and how to burn. Unfortunately, his cock was bowed and penetration was always painful. I tried and tried to find a position that could work, to no avail. It was the primary reason I stopped being his lover, and I never told him why. It wasn't anything he could change. I still remember him with love.

The following semester I moved to Westwood to take some extension classes at UCLA and audit whatever classes interested me. I was on my own, waitressing to survive. My father never encouraged me to further my education and could not afford to put his six kids through college, though I know he helped Kate. The rest of us were left to fend for ourselves. He wanted me to marry and have lots of children because he believed I would be happy. The thought of taking on the role my mother had been saddled with was unbearable to me. My journey was mine alone, and I would find what I was looking for or die trying.

*

I met Khaled while hitchhiking down Westwood Boulevard.

Later he called having found my wallet in his car. He dropped it off and asked if I would come to dinner at his home. I was impressed with his honesty and figured it was little enough to accept in return for the kindness he'd shown me.

Khaled was a handsome man, sent by his hero Muammar Gaddafi to get a PhD in P.E. in order to head up that department of Gaddafi's government. I never watched the news in those days.

I did not own a television and knew nothing of the troubled Middle East. Khaled was intent upon changing that as he welcomed me graciously into his home. He spoke to me about the importance of hospitality in his culture. As his guest, if I wanted anything, I need not even ask. I could just go to the refrigerator and take whatever I desired.

"My home is yours," he said. He had invited two of his male friends to the dinner he prepared that night. It was a delicious stew made with chunks of beef heart in a savory tomato sauce, cooked all day to achieve the tenderness.

He was shocked to see me pick up the fork with my left hand and begin to eat. "What are you doing?" he asked, as if on the edge of rage.

"What do you mean?" I responded.

"We don't eat with our left hand, we use that to wipe our ass," the gentleman announced.

I was dumbfounded. I attempted to switch hands, and he quickly recovered his manners begrudgingly saying, "It's okay, it makes us sick to watch but as you are the guest, you may do as you wish." It was the first indication that this would not go well.

Khaled quickly turned the conversation toward my education. "Do you know, if there is a World War III, why it will be?" I didn't bother to tell him I'd never questioned or considered it, only hoped that it would never be.

"It will be because of the 200,000 Palestinian refugees that were driven out of their homes, bulldozed down to the ground by the Jews. And these refugees were not merely poor peasants; they were doctors, lawyers, engineers, professors, and professionals of all sorts, mercilessly cast out of their own land!"

He then regaled me with stories of Libya's glorious leader Gaddafi, the revolting, deplorable, maniac! Khaled manned the PLO booth on the main pathway of campus where it seemed everyone had something to prove. He gave me a copy of the PLO's manifesto, a small 75-page book describing the takedown of Palestine. It was my first inside view of the Palestinian plight and would leave me with a sense of having a foot on either side of the fence for a long time.

Odd that it was he who inadvertently led me to the Israelis. On one of our very few dates, we went to a place called "The Seventh Veil". It was a nightclub on Sunset, where the Arabs and the Israelis sat at separate tables enjoying the Middle Eastern music they both loved. I was immediately drawn to the other side of the room, though I did not yet know how much of my life would be forever filled with Israelis and Israel.

When Khaled's friends left that night, we had sex and that's all it was. It was another first for me, discovering what it was like to try to make love to a man who was raised to regard women as beneath him. There seemed to be no idea or intention to please the woman. On the contrary, a woman who could take pleasure in the sex act would likely be considered a whore. I had, however, already become an irresistible, albeit insatiable, lover. And he, as with the others, would be back for more until I stopped him.

I invited him over for a sumptuous dinner one night, introducing him to my roommate Eleanor Weinstein. Later we romped again in the living room. When he was finished, he got up and wandered into the back room where Eleanor was studying. I waited maybe five minutes. Then I got up, went to the front door where he had left his shoes, picked them up, and called out, "Oh Khaled, I think you forgot your shoes!" With that, I opened the door and chucked his shoes down the stairs, just in time for him to see me do it and run after them. I slammed the door behind him as hard as I could.

Eleanor came out of the back room and simply said in her feisty way, "Because they cannot beat us on the battlefield, they try to bed our women." Oddly, I didn't know at that time, I too am a Jew.

I called Khaled the next day to be sure it was over. He said, "Only one other person ever threw me out of their house, and that was my father." It was over.

I ran the gamut of lovers, mostly one-night stands. There was one day when I had a bearded biker in the afternoon and a blond hippie boy that night. Then I knew I was bad. The biker accused me of using him for sex when I refused to see him again. He was right.

And then came the priest. Father 'Patrick' (not his real name) was a Jesuit teacher at Kate and Lorin's high school and was regarded with respect by our family. When my oldest brother was planning to marry, he asked me if I would get in touch with Patrick and ask him to perform the ceremony.

At the time Patrick was dean of a Catholic boys' high school. I made an appointment and arrived early. I decided to check out the school's church. In the dimly lit shadows,

I wandered toward the back and up the stairs to the choir loft, so much like the ones I'd spent my childhood singing in. I stared across the pews at the sanctuary, sensing the emptiness that now filled me.

I wanted to commit some sacrilege to prove that the Church was no longer a sanctuary for me. I slipped my hand down my pants, gliding my fingers into my slit. I was soon wet and writhing in the choir loft, coming hard.

In all fairness, I was probably still glowing when I entered Patrick's office. We'd barely spoken three sentences before he was pulling off my pants and going down on me on his office floor. Then he spirited me away to his room in the rectory, where we continued the sex. Pretty sure the excitement was more that I was "doing it" with a priest than his prowess.

I was a little surprised when he called later for a date. At dinner in Impresario's, he made a comment that insured it would be his last. We were having a lovely meal overlooking the city before the concert. He looked across the table at me and said, "You and your sister could get a man to do anything for you. The difference is that Kate smiles and makes you happy to do it." I wasn't sure where that was coming from except that I had already imagined he wished he'd had a chance to make it with her. I decided then and there that he would never have the chance to make it with me again.

Years later, Kate called me to ask if I'd seen the article about Patrick in The New York Times. Apparently, the good Father had an affair many years ago with a fifteen-year-old girl on their high school debate team for which he was the advisor. He had continued to send her letters through the years, hoping that she would still think kindly of him. She was married with children and never responded but eventually got fed up and contacted the archdiocese. She was awarded an untold sum for the continued harassment. Turned out he doesn't do weddings.

Eventually I met Chris. He had graduated the year before with a BA in Art History. He was gorgeous, and I thought I could gaze upon that face all my life and be satisfied.

We moved in together, and every Sunday we would have brunch at The Egg and the Eye. Afterwards we would go to LACMA, a contemporary art museum in the heart of L.A., and he would walk me through hall after hall, floor after floor, teaching me everything he knew about art.

Today I can enter any museum in the world and recognize many of the artists on the walls. For this and the introduction he gave me to Nietzsche and my favorite poet Arthur Rimbaud, I am ever grateful to him.

Unfortunately, in the year or more that we lived together, I came only once. Extraordinary, because I could come using only my imagination! Then he refused to repeat what he had done to make me come.

It got so bad that one night when he fell asleep, I left and went searching for a friend of mine, who was living and studying down the street at the Chabad House. I went around the back, climbed up the trellis to the second floor, and ducked into his open window. We had sex, and then I spirited away after extracting a promise from him to keep our secret.

I told Chris about it sometime later, naively thinking if he realized I wasn't satisfied he'd be willing to work on it. He wasn't. He was in shock that he'd been cuckolded. I was weeping, begging him to forgive me, when I suddenly remembered that Yarosha had asked me to go and see his Teacher speak that day. I called him, choking back the tears as I declined the invitation. It would be years before that opportunity would come again.

Chris moved out. I went to see him at his new place. He refused to open the door. I kicked it down. It didn't help. It just scared him. I am not so sure if I actually wanted him back or just didn't want him to be the first to leave. In the end, I let him go and have never seen him again. I hope he is well. As for me, it seemed I was well-suited to being alone, and I fell in love with my aloneness.

*

By the time I started studying with O, I was working a forty-hour week, plus the fifteen hours with him and whatever classes I was auditing. My time for socializing was narrowing.

I took a place in a large Hollywood house that had been broken up into several ample-sized apartments, where O also lived. My space was around the back garden. It had a big front room with wood floors that I left empty to use as a studio. The kitchen and bathroom were also a good size but the bedroom was extremely narrow. It just barely accommodated a full-size mattress, leaving no room on either side. Behind the bed a louvered window filled the wall. I often fell asleep in my clothes with all the windows open and the door unlocked. I was in the habit of continuing to work until I could no longer keep my eyes open.

One night I was awakened in the darkness by a stranger straddled on his knees across my waist, pinning my wrists down on either side of my shoulders. At first, I thought it was my friend Susan from O's class, who lived in the apartment above me, playing some trick on me. She had curly hair like a bush, and that was all I could see now. I reached up and touched the hair. This kinky coarse hair was not Susan's. The next thing I noticed was his smell.

I had too many times thought only a foolish woman would prefer to be killed rather than raped. No longer. It is interesting how solidly aware I was in that moment. O was sleeping in his own apartment on the other side of my bedroom wall, but I dared not scream. Instead, I tried lying to gain his sympathy.

"Please, I am sickly. You may take whatever you want, but you may not take me!"

"Shut up!" he whispered in a low tone. He had already taken what little cash I had.

I had not really prayed in a long time but I prayed now. I cried out softly for God to help me because clearly only He could. "Oh, dear God, please help me."

To which the stranger retorted, "Shut up! I am not listening to you."

I persisted, "God help me, please help me!"

"Shut up, I am not listening to you."

I began to notice that each time I prayed he loosened his grip on my wrists. I saw I could use this to my advantage. The only way off the bed was towards the foot of it, as the walls blocked me on either side. So I continued to pray, somehow adjusting my position each time, slowly but surely.

All the while he continued ranting, "Shut up, I am not listening to you!"

Then, miraculously, we were both at edge of the bed. I called upon every ounce of courage within me and managed to stand up with him still holding onto my wrists. Then I started walking backwards, leading him out of my bedroom and into the barren front room.

Now, though he was still holding onto me, it was me who was controlling him. I backed us up to the door and broke free of his grip using a release technique that I would later be formally taught in Kung Fu. I backed away to the center of the room, as he stood there transfixed by the door.

"Now if you don't leave, I will scream. I am giving you five minutes to get away before I call the police."

"Okay, I'm going." And he walked out the door.

*

As Chloe and I tromped through the streets of Wrocław, I didn't offer the story of that experience with the intruder. I kept it for myself. I could not bring my victimhood here and achieve my goal. I needed all my power. And besides it was not in my nature to offer negative information about myself without some constructive purpose. As open as others believed me to be, I was almost entirely hidden and would remain an extremely private person until now. That need for exclusion would show itself in my inability to merge with a group, making ensemble work nearly impossible, and only now do I realize it.

About thirty of us from around the world between the ages of 19-40 gathered that night at The Theater Laboratory. We waited in a white-walled room on the second floor to be interviewed by Spizalszki, the man that had been appointed by Grotowski to direct the Rencontres Preliminaires that year.

I was amazed and a little ashamed as I watched and listened to the Europeans chatting back and forth across the room, each speaking several languages at once and understanding all! Then a young woman from New York City burst back into the waiting room totally exasperated and incensed. "He told me to leave when I told him I'd left my two children back home with my husband!"

With each ensuing interview, they dropped like flies. Then my turn came to climb the staircase, just one flight up to the small room where Spizalszki awaited.

I entered with some trepidation. He asked me to tell him about myself. I said I'd been struggling with sadness all my life because I was looking for something I'd not yet found.

He retorted, "There is no heroism in sadness, anyone can be sad. It takes a hero to happy." For a split second I figured I was done for, and then he said, "See you on the first night." I smiled, thanked him, and leapt back down the stairs, silently rejoicing.

One by one, we made our way to the town discotheque called Pauwatzic. The coat check woman thought it'd be cute to teach me a couple of Polish phrases like "Ja jestem zwarjowana", which means "I am a crazy woman", and "Pocałuj mnie w dupe", which means "Kiss my ass". I found both phrases really did come in handy.

I joined Chloe at her table. She had been told that because she had just worked with Grotowski in the south of France making "Holiday" with Grot's actors, she was ineligible to join the Rencontre Preliminaire but she could join the "Stage Theorique" group.

"Holiday" was a new form of encounter that Grotowski was experimenting with in the forests. He took the participants to the extremes of their trust, breaking all human barriers to bring forth an explosion of ecstatic energy from within. Chloe said, "I burned in 'Holiday'. I must find a way to burn again!"

I ordered a brandy and hot tea. No sooner had I taken the first sip of brandy when Wiesław walked up. He was a young man with kind brown eyes and a sweet round face softly framed by his brown hair.

He knelt beside me on one knee and slurring his words just a little said, "Please don't drink. You are with the Theatre, yes?"

I nodded.

"Then please don't drink! The people know you are with the Theatre. If you drink, it will not be good for you and it will not be good for Grotowski!"

Normally I did not take instructions from anyone, but I looked at him and felt his sincerity. He was earnest, and I was inclined not to disappoint him, despite the fact that it was clear he had been drinking steadily! I did not take another sip.

I learned that he too had once worked in the Theatre. Emmanuelle joined us. I introduced her to Wiesław. He soon fell in love with her. We all got on the stage and began to dance. There too was someone with a suggestion. It was Olaf, a friend of Wiesław, as well as a former member of the Theatre. "Be free. Dance your own dance."

I stopped doing the Twist and began to explore the freedom of movement. It was all at once fun and liberating. In the frenzy of the dance, there is a kind of intoxication.

I saw a boy, younger than myself, maybe seventeen. He was blond with pink lips. Not usually my type, but I wound up in his bedroom. I had sex with him and then found my way back to the home where I was staying.

When he came looking for me at the Theatre the next day, I tried to be gentle as I dismissed him. He gave me a small picture of himself to remember him by. I still have it.

I had gone back into the center of town that day and wandered into a large church. It was one of so many I might have chosen to visit, as there seemed to be a church on every other block. It was the fashion there for centuries for rich nobles to build churches on their property in hopes of saving their souls. Now it was my soul in need of saving.

I entered the church with reluctance. I had not been in one for a long time. I stood in the back aisle amidst the shadows surrounding me. Only faint light filtered through the ancient windows. I refused to kneel but prayed nonetheless, imploring God once again.

"Please, I am begging you. Help me! Let me find the missing piece I've searched for, for so long." Tears ran down my cheeks. I wiped them away and walked back out into the square with resolve.

Olaf had invited us all to his home for a gathering that night. Seems like Wiesław was always around as a tipsy guardian angel shadowing us. It was he who encouraged me to come along. I was often reluctant to attend parties, preferring to be alone. And especially as this was the night before The Encounter would begin. But Wiesław was almost impossible to say no to. There was something so dear and innocent about him, I felt compelled to give in to his insistent requests. So after eating an ice cream sundae, one of the best I've ever tasted and a favorite of Poles in the cold winters, I tagged along with Emmanuelle and Wiesław to Olaf's gathering.

Olaf was a tall young man with bright red hair. He was kind, compassionate, and had sage advice that would later prove to be invaluable for me.

About half the candidates were there, and everyone seemed to enjoy getting to know one another. There was MM, from Andre Gregory's Performance Group; Maroshiro from Japan; and a cheerful, chubby American girl named Jackie, among others.

I still had a purple scar across my right cheek from the fall in Paris. I suspected it scared people but they probably would have been afraid of me anyway. I was obviously not someone to be played with.

Later that night, a girl came into the party and announced that Spizalszki was also having a gathering of some of the participants and Grotowski was there. Several of Olaf's guests, myself included, decided that it might be more advantageous to go to Spizalszki's place. The chance to share a casual and intimate moment with Grot was too enticing to pass up.

I have never forgotten the look of painful disappointment in Olaf's eyes as I left that night, and all for nothing. When we arrived at Spizalszki's, the party was over, Grot had left, and we looked like idiots! I had failed the test of loyalty to my friend, and it would be a lesson I'd never forget.

The next day was the first of The Encounter, scheduled to begin at 9 pm. Everyone was dressed in the theatre garb of the day—casual, comfortable, and somewhat form-fitting but not enough to impede movement. We were led up to the top floor of the Theatre Lab, where the magnificent workspace awaited us. The exceptionally large room had walls painted black, a parquet floor, and the feeling of sanctuary. I was prepared to lay down my life to become part of this Theatre. I had spent two years preparing, tirelessly attempting to master the exercises that I knew were a part of Grot's experimentation.

Grotowski was considered to be the greatest director of avant-garde theatre in the world. He had been invited by Peter Brook to give a workshop at the Royal Shakespeare Academy. Andre Gregory would devote an entire film to his work with Grot called *My Dinner with Andre*. I often quipped that if Jung were alive, I would have gone to him, but as he wasn't, I went to Grotowski.

I had first met Grot when he arrived in Los Angeles as a guest of Ossetynski, having been invited to speak at the Mark Taper Forum. I was intrigued by him. When he walked into a room, his genius preceded him. I had never felt such an intense presence before. He was quite thin, dressed entirely in black as was his custom. His straggly brown hair and beard were unkempt. I was glued to his every breath. The focus of my concentration was such that what started as respect began to resemble love. The very nearness of him was exciting for me, not sexually but somehow romantically. I knew I needed to work with him in order to find for myself the mystery he had unveiled.

I was privileged to sit in on small exclusive gatherings in O's salon, where Grotowski was taking questions, discussing his life and work. When he spoke, each word was a sound dropping into my heart.

Ossetynski commented to him about me, "She has difficulty with discipline."

Grot retorted, "La discipline est une formalite" ("Discipline is a formality").

I told him, faltering in my speech, "Je veux venir étudier le théâtre avec vous" ("I want to come to study theater with you").

To which he simply said, "Bienvenue" ("Welcome").

We entered the room with a kind of solemnity. A few of the guys were asked to carry in a guitar, tablas, and a steel washbasin large enough to hold a small person.

We were instructed to form a circle along the walls. Spizalszki took his position. Grotowski came in shortly thereafter, taking a seat against the back wall.

After welcoming us, Spizalszki suggested that we each find a way of introducing ourselves, and there was no restriction given at that point as to how. I was taken aback for a moment, having nothing prepared.

Maroshiro got up and performed an electrifying set of Kung Fu. It was beautiful and offered great insight into his character. When my turn came, I had settled on performing the first segment of the solo masterpiece I'd been working on from Arthur Rimbaud's *Season in Hell*:

"Yesterday, if my memory serves me, my life was a banquet where everyone's heart was generous and all wines flowed. One evening I pulled beauty down upon my knees. I found her embittered and I cursed her. I took arms against justice. I ran away. Oh witches, poverty, hate—I have confided my treasure to you! I was able to expel from my mind all human hope. On every form of joy, in order to strangle it, I pounced stealthily like a wild animal. I called to my executioners to let me bite the ends of their guns as I died. I called to all plagues to stifle me with sand and blood. Disaster was my god. I stretched out in mud. I dried myself in criminal air. I played clever

tricks on insanity. Spring brought me to an idiot's terrifying laughter. But recently, on the verge of giving my last croak, I thought of looking for the key to the ancient banquet where I might possibly recover my appetite. Charity is the key. This lofty thought proves I dreamt it!"

It was appropriate coming from me, though I wasn't certain about my performance, and there were no do-overs.

When everyone had finished, we were given instructions. First, avoid talking or singing of any kind unless it was absolutely necessary to the content of The Encounter. Then, "Music should exist throughout and those not playing the music should exist vis à vis la musique."

And lastly, an admonition not to discuss what transpires here with anyone ever. And though I know the passage of time has not released me from that commitment, I feel the importance of my discovery as it relates to this story, does.

Grotowski then got up and left. It was a surprise to me that he was handing over the directive reins for this encounter to someone else, let alone this man I knew nothing about. I was sure Grot was somewhere watching when he wasn't in the room with us. How could he resist? His life's work was based on the experimentation that took place within these walls.

Then with a slight lift of Spizalszki's hands, all were on their feet, and a march began. Each of us had at our disposal our own history, our talents, and our training. Our bodies were our instruments, our breath the force of life within us. Our stifled voices might have more meaning in grunts and sighs. Our eyes became the expression of our souls. On this first night, we began as if we were cavemen struggling to come up with a system of communication. I

82

saw my quandary: act within the group or be ostracized or even self-exiled.

The night was long and arduous. By the end, I wasn't sure where I was or what I'd accomplished. It was hours after midnight when we finished and wandered wordlessly out onto the snow-packed streets in the cold night air. Most of the participants were staying in a dormitory-type barracks on the edge of the forest just outside town. I was one of the few with private lodgings. I stood alone in the taxi line, wondering how there were people ahead of me at 3 am!

The next day, I went into town early and ran into Olaf, who asked me how I was feeling. I used my thumb and my forefinger to show something small and said, "I feel about this far from nothing."

He walked along beside me thoughtfully.

"And what does it mean to you when someone asks you to repeat something?"

"It means to do it again," I asserted confidently.

"To begin again," Olaf responded poignantly, looking directly in my eyes to press his point. "Yes?" he said, checking my understanding. Then he offered me some solid, practical advice. "Tonight, don't stop moving and don't shut eyes. Because when you sitting, you thinking. Don't think. Just fly!"

That night in The Encounter I remembered what he told me. I entered the work determined to keep moving. The group quickly began where we'd left off the night before. The history of the human race seemed to be forming. Animal characters were introduced and began to flourish. I became a leaping frog against the beat of the tabla. I jumped high up into the air. Then down, slamming my hands on the floor with webbed palms and springing back up higher, then down harder and up higher until I felt as if I would asphyxiate myself should I move just one tiny finger. I went beyond my concern and experienced a blast of energy, a "second wind".

The washbasin became a boat, a seat to carry someone, perhaps an ailing pauper or a new king. I continued to engage in any way I could, letting myself merge with the group and be carried into the creation of the whole as it morphed into a massive display of undocumented drama. I became so fully engaged that I couldn't breathe, but I was determined not to stop moving. I would continue even at the risk of death, and again the burst of blessed energy came allowing me to continue, almost as if it was urging me on.

The guitar strings began to sing in the background. I was now performing an African native dance, jumping high in the air, squatting down deep and again the leap in ecstasy. Then came the moment I felt, "This is it, you will die." Instead, a great wind rushed under me, and I was lifted off the ground by a huge wave that swept me backwards some 30 feet to the other end of the room. I found myself tossed helplessly like a thin flag rippling in the mighty wind, submerged in a radiant golden ocean of light and energy! It was spectacular, beyond anything I had ever imagined. And it took all of my conscious power to pull myself out of that ocean and back into my body.

It was then that I saw Maroshiro worshiping at my feet. I backed away—first to the wall and then out of the room. Spizalszki made no motion as I crossed his path on my way out the door. I went to the waiting room and looked in the mirror to be sure I was still there. I was there, all right, stunned speechless and suddenly terrified. If this was the power of light, how great could the opposing darkness be? I returned to the room now with cautious anticipation.

It was 5 am when I took my place at end of the taxi line that morning. I felt an exhilaration I had never known before. For the first time in my life, I was aware that I was somehow glowing, a smile perched upon my face. Warmed from within, the subzero weather seemed just brisk. I literally crawled up the four flights of stairs to the flat. I now knew what Grot had meant when he said you know the difference between lazy and tired in the cells of your being. Nothing would ever be the same for me. This night my life quaked and changed forever. My pursuit now would be to get back to that feeling of overwhelming light. I was enthralled by the beauty and wished only to dance upon the crest of a wave in that ocean. I knew I had to find my way back, but how?

When I returned to the theatre the next night I noticed before we began that the guitar was splattered with blood. Someone had played it until his fingers bled. The Encounter continued every night for two weeks without a break. I tried night after night to jump back into that light. I gave myself over to reckless abandon, to no avail. More and more discouraged, one night I worked myself into a froth and then a frenzy, still to no avail. Instead I found myself flapping around on the floor. I was floundering like a dying fish in the darkness. Spizalszki actually got up to stop me. "If you continue like that, it will only lead to hysteria and then you will be crying alone!"

Sometime later I wrote to a friend about the experience.

It is in the night sea
when the eyes are shut
that motion becomes madness
I have tried
and yet see no place for resolution
in that which entices all the senses.
What resolve at the stake,
leaves burning an aura of dawn
in deep night?

It is through the mask to the shore
where lies the wild frontier
of immeasurable beauty,
then everything is dropped into the will,
which is left on the sand,
and the entire being is overcome
on a voyage of creation towards light
or was that re–creation towards being?

I spent hours in the day walking through the forest as if searching for some answer. What was I doing wrong, how was I missing it? How could I make it happen again? My focus had gone completely off the group and onto my own obsession, though only now do I see it. In the night's work, while the others clung together, I was growing more distant. It was in this time that I started hanging out more with Wiesław. He loved jazz and was fond of Bob Dylan, as well as the Beatles. We would sing together whenever we could: "Blowin' in the Wind", "Times They Are a Changin'", and "Blackbird" were among the songs. But "Dona Dona" was, I think, his favorite.

We sat and talked in real bars and milk bars, enjoying our fantastic lives. I was lucky to have dollars to trade with grandmothers in their kitchens. Black market trading was an offense punishable by death in Russia, but apparently not so serious in Poland. Due to the extraordinary rate of exchange, for the first time in my life, I was rich and I enjoyed taking six people out to a six-course meal for $1.25.

Wiesław often entertained us at these dinners with the stories of his many adventures. Because he gave himself totally to the pursuit of enjoying life, there was no shortage of tales to tell. He had been the doorkeeper of Grotowski's Apocalypsis cum Figuris. I was never quite sure what that meant. I assumed it meant he stood outside the door as a guard.

Grot, though supported by the Russian Communists, did not allow them in to see his work. I had the impression that Grot allowed Wiesław to work in the theatre at some point. He was clearly the beloved town drunk, and though I did not really understand him at the time, I enjoyed his company.

Wiesław was incapable of harsh judgment. He told me his mother had died when he was just a boy, and ever since then he had taken cold showers even in the dead of winter. It was a penance of some sort, though he never explained why. Strangely enough, when I was twelve I too was in the practice of taking cold showers as a form of contrition in the hope of gaining Plenary indulgences. But I abandoned that when I abandoned my father's religion.

I assumed at the time that Wiesław felt guilty about his mother's death as so many do when a loved one passes. Or perhaps it was a sacrifice offered to save her soul. I suppose that privately romanticizing it was better than prying for answers, especially since Wiesław held back very little. I wish now that I had asked him.

The Encounter was coming to a close. I had struggled to return to that ocean of light, not realizing how rare it was to have stumbled onto it even once. I had no idea how many of the others had experienced it in that particular Encounter, if any. I still think it could only have been a few.

The day came for posting the list of those who would be invited to stay on at the theatre for a six-month term. Spizalszki had told us the night before at the end of the last session that those not on the list could request a meeting with him but not to be hopeful. That's just the way it is in theater and in love. If someone loves you or if they do not love you, they cannot tell you why.

The list went up. There were only five people on it including MM, Maroshiro, and only one woman, Jackie, the cheerful chubby girl who was wild and strong. My name was not there, much to my deep sorrow and distress. The sense of failure was overwhelming. I did request a meeting with Spizalszki, a man I had never felt even a little bit close to. As if protesting my dismissal, I told him of my experience in the ocean. Surely, I had achieved something. He simply said it should have been a calling to the others to join in. But, for me it had been an entirely individual and personal experience that I was a long way from understanding.

I stopped by Ludwig Flaszen's office on my way out. He was the technical director of the theatre and he had an intriguing observation for me, "It is this air of sadness that condemns you. You must rid yourself of the judge that rests within you."

*

Since I was not staying, I wanted to leave immediately. We all met that night for a farewell party at Pauwatzic. I sat at a table near the dance floor—nothing to stop me from drinking now. I ordered tea and the brandy I'd abstained from before, when suddenly Wiesław appeared again. He already knew I was leaving and he was very sad. He carried in his hands a large wad of newspaper. He handed it to me with tears in his eyes.

"Open it," he said.

Bewildered, I gingerly opened the sheets of newsprint to discover his prized jean jacket with knitted flowers sewn over the worn areas. I had admired it once, and now he was giving to me as a parting gift to remember him by. The thing is it was his only jacket, and it was still the dead of winter. I tried to gently refuse it but an angry expression washed over his face and he insisted. To refuse it then would have been an insult. So I thanked him, hugged him, and put it on.

I got quite drunk that night and wound up wandering in the forest with MM. I said, "To the victor goes the spoils!" And we fucked on the forest floor for no reason. When we got up, we were both covered with mud from head to toe. We realized we could not return to our respective residences in that condition, so we agreed to spend the rest of the night in a hotel called the Orbis. It catered to Americans, and though we were a sight to be seen, we whipped out our American passports at the front desk and unbelievably were given a room. We bathed and slept separately. There was nothing between us. In the morning, we went our separate ways.

I had agreed to meet Wiesław in town the next day. He had promised to take me to the train station. There I was standing in the middle of the town with all my bags around my feet. My duffel bag alone must have weighed 80 pounds.

Wiesław entreated me to stay. "Please come with us to Zakopane in the mountains. Emmanuelle is coming. You can rest there, relax, have fun, and then go if you must!" Emmanuelle stood by him, quietly observing without interfering as was often her way. His eyes welled up with penetrating sadness.

"I can't stay. I have to go. I must go," I insisted. I would not be dissuaded.

My rejection from The Theatre Laboratory was so humiliating that I couldn't face another day there. And, as usual, I was blind to the kindness and acceptance of my friends. I could not leave quickly enough. Dutifully and without another word, Wiesław hoisted my duffel bag onto his back and ran down the track to catch the trolley we had just missed. Night had already fallen as we hopped on the halted trolley together, headed for the train station.

Wiesław reached into his pocket, pulled out some cash, and gave it to the engineer, instructing him to go directly to the train station without making any stops. He did not want me to leave, but he was willing to do anything in his power to help me. Emmanuelle sat silent beside me. Wiesław took a seat across from us. When the ticket taker came by for the ticket stubs we did not have, Wiesław waved her away. It was Communist Poland, and everyone who was employed remained so whether they took their job seriously or not. And besides the ticket money was for the Communists not them.

Wiesław took periodic swigs from the whiskey bottle he had illegally brought onto the trolley with him. Then he hid the bottle behind his legs and singing softly in Polish, rocking back and forth, pounded out the beat of the song with his hands on his thighs as he wept copiously.

I looked at him and suddenly I saw him. A dear sweet human being so full of the great compassion that I was so incapable of. I realized I had never really seen a human being before. I had never been able to. There he sat weeping over losing his callous friend, and in him I saw humanity. It stunned me. Amazingly, in some way, the effect was even more profound than the plunge into the ocean of light and energy that had rocked me weeks before. Had that experience somehow changed me? Made me ready to see? Until then, I thought I'd seen it all.

I began to weep. Wiesław saw my tears and said sternly, "Don't cry!" and again more forcefully when I could not stop, "Don't cry! Not now!" He resumed his lamentation as I gazed at him in wonder. Strange, he was bawling but I was not to cry for he could not bear that I would also weep.

We arrived at the station only to discover that the last train for Paris had left long before.

Again Wiesław asked, "Are you sure you still want to leave?"

Sadly, I said, "Yes, I'm sure." He did not argue.

"Okay, so tonight you come to my home to stay and tomorrow if you still want, I will bring you back here."

I nodded. "Okay," I said, "Thank you so much. I'm sorry I can't stay."

"It's okay," he said with reassuring sincerity.

When we arrived at Wiesław's home, it seemed everyone was asleep. He offered me tea and something to eat, then off to his room, where he gave me his bed. He would take the floor. I slipped comfortably under the covers and settled in. Wiesław picked up the edge of the feather comforter and began shaking it up and down, higher and higher until it was fluffed three feet deep. Then he sat down on the floor beside the bed saying with a smile, "My mother used to do that for me."

"Tell me about her," I asked. His eyes welled up with tears as he reminisced about the beautiful mother he had missed for so long. Just then, as if on cue, a large imposing woman entered the room to ask if we needed anything.

He said to his stepmother, "Nie, jiekuje" ("No, thank you"). With that, she left us alone.

"She seems nice."

Wiesław shrugged his shoulders. "Once a friend of mine who was in trouble asked if he could stay here a few days. Before he went, he had left a box under my bed. My stepmother discovered it. Turned out to be a heroin kit. I did not know it was there. She thought it was mine and called the police. They arrested me, took me to jail, and beat me continuously all weekend, trying to get me to give them my friend's name. But I would not. When they finally let me go, it was to a hospital to recover." That was Wiesław: brave, loyal, and true to the end.

In the morning, he took me back to the station. As I looked deeply into his warm brown eyes, promising to return, he said with great kindness and wisdom, "You must go and look for where your heart is."

We hugged one last time, and I left for Paris.

Chapter Five — JM

When I boarded the train to Paris that night, I searched for an empty cabin but could find none. I settled on the one with an empty seat by the door. All the other five seats were taken by men dressed in the Polish version of a cheap business suit. They must've had some stature to be allowed to travel out of Poland, though only now does it occur to me that they got off in East Germany. I quickly placed my duffel bag and a smaller suitcase in the upper berth and took my seat as the train began to move.

Before leaving Warsaw, I had been asked by family friends of Ossetynski to bring a large piece of amber for their daughter who was studying in California. They could not send money and probably did not have any. They cautioned me that it was illegal to take the amber out of the country and that if I were caught, I would be arrested.

"No problem," I told them. I was happy to do it.

I suppose I thought a little adventure on my way out of the country would be fun. So I had stashed the oval-shaped stone into my narrow vaginal canal where it could remain safely undiscovered without a cavity search. I had packed in my suitcase two vases glazed in a brilliant blue enamel that were also forbidden to be taken out of the country.

Imagine my surprise when the train stopped at the East German border and the guards came in throwing everyone's luggage into the hallway, cabin after cabin. I looked out the door of the cabin and saw the valises were open on the floor just several cabins down the way, and clothes were strewn everywhere. I sat back down and closed my eyes. If they found the vases in my suitcase, I was in trouble, and the amber would surely be next! So I did what I normally do in such situations—I fell asleep instantly.

Then suddenly the train began to move again, and the jostling of it woke me. At that point one of the men in the cabin, who with the others had been watching my curious behavior, looked at me and said, "Now we want to see what you have been hiding."

Thank goodness I had something to show them without disrobing! I jumped up, lifted down my suitcase from above, and showed them the vases. Ah! Then they understood. She is sneaking out the vases!

Once we were in East Germany, the mood became far less frivolous. No one spoke. Each man read their own newspaper and barely glanced at one another, let alone me. Complete silence. Clearly, they were afraid of something— a stranger in their midst, perhaps. One never knew who might be listening.

I kept to myself, scratching down a few thoughts:

I sense in the distance
there is something, I don't know what or where
that awaits me. I search for it.
I have tasted a new and wild frontier
the universe beyond the mask.
I must re-find it.

When I arrived in Paris at Gare de l'Est, there was no one to greet me. Only Madame knew I was returning. I had called her from Poland and told her I was coming back, just casually. She was delighted. She quickly forgave me for leaving her in the lurch, as it were, and told me she was dissatisfied with the girl she'd hired in my place.

"Just come," she said, "your room will be waiting for you!"

I was truly grateful and relieved. I dragged my heavy duffel bag up the seven flights of spiral staircases, stumbled back into my room, and plopping down on the bed, I wept for a while.

In the morning, I got in touch with Jean. The thought that I'd been unfaithful to him never entered my mind. Jean was sad to see me, not because he didn't want me, just that he knew what The Theater Laboratory meant to me.

There was no sugar coating it. I had failed. I had reached an unimaginable illumination and still somehow failed. Where was the door? Why could I not get back? Jean would soon realize I had never really returned. I was journey-bound to find my way back to my ocean of light and energy.

Jean got an idea. It was to take me away to a friend's family manor house far into the country. I agreed, thinking perhaps it would relax me.

We took a train past Reims, disembarking in what seemed to be the middle of nowhere. Dusk was upon us as we headed out on foot to the manor house. It turned out to be several miles away. Night fell and stars filled the sky. That was our only light, except for the tiny villages glistening in the distance.

I recall being a pain about the long walk. It was a bit eerie, walking on that dark road beneath the magnificent dome of the starlit sky. Still I trusted Jean would get us there, and he did.

Once we arrived, I learned that he didn't actually have the key. And the spare was not so quickly findable. But somehow Jean found a way in. He switched on the light. We entered through a kitchen large enough for a full working staff.

We were quite hungry, and as no one had been there in a while, there was little to eat. We found only crackers and tuna, which we consumed unceremoniously. Still, it was all so beautiful. Jean seemed to know his way around the place. He led me up to the master bedroom by candlelight. It was complete with a four-poster bed. We crawled in and kept each other warm until morning.

In the dawn's light, we were treated to a sunlit view of the manor's many rooms. The salon was beautifully appointed with ample windows facing the garden. A magnificent ornate mantel topped the stone fireplace that stood at one end of the room. A large wingback stuffed leather chair sat beside it. I made a mental note, I will park myself there later.

Jean and I headed into the village to get some staples: bread, cheese, and butter. The villagers were remarkably friendly. I immediately noticed how different they were in comparison to the Parisians. And they seemed to know Jean though he had told me it was the vacation home of a friend's family. All that had seemed so frightening in the night was now charming and full of sunshine, almost glimmering, like a Van Gogh painting.

We took our wonderfully fresh bread and cheese back to the manor's kitchen, along with a bar of chocolate, from which Jean would make my favorite cocoa for dessert. I made coffee first. Then we enjoyed a perfect petit dèjeuner! There was little, if any, chatter. Jean knew I needed rest and reflection. And there was nothing to say. It never occurred to me or to Jean that I would not remain at The Theater Laboratory.

The chill of winter still hung in the air. "I'll make a fire," Jean said and got up quickly.

Plopping myself down on that overstuffed chair, I opened the book I'd brought along. It was Dear Theo, Van Gogh's letters to his brother. I was enjoying them, but it occurred to me that letters sent and received hold no promise of privacy, especially after death. That idea deeply troubled me, as privacy has always been very important to me.

Closing the book, I watched out the window a few moments, my attention drawn by the sound of chopping wood. It was Jean, in all his manly elegance, chopping logs on a tree stump with his beautiful muscular arms. He would have a huge fire warming me soon enough. I reached for my journal and began a letter to Chloe. My journals would always be full of letters never sent.

Dear Chloe,

I am passing a few days in a country house outside Paris.

Jean brought me. He must have realized I was in need of rest.

My arrival in Paris was somewhat grim, as reality tends to be at times. Everything has changed between Jean and me. We're not really looking for the same things in life. The needs we once fulfilled for one another no longer exist.

I leave for the Alps in a few weeks to work as an au pair at the chalet of my old patron, Madame. After Poland I cannot tolerate the wet climate of France. Perhaps the mountain air will be more agreeable to me, until spring.

I feel a strong need to return to my own country in search of others with whom I could work, in the hope that we might take off over the ocean on an endless voyage, constantly stripping from ourselves everything that gives weight to the inane and makes heavy what might otherwise be light. I long to be pulled again into that feeling where the sea meets the sun. It is everything I want from living.

scorched,

me

We went back to Paris that night, somewhat unexpectedly. My queries to Jean regarding our sudden departure were met with vague reasons and shrugged shoulders. Had I dozed off in the chair, journal open to the letter on my lap?

There was a letter from Susan, my dear friend in O's class, waiting for me upon my return. We had been studying together for years and she seemed to almost worship Ossetynski. He was certainly deserving of respect, but worship? Not from me, but then I wasn't in love with him, and she surely was. He knew of her devotion and used it to his full advantage. In all fairness, she was thirsty for all she could learn from him despite the fact that she had long ago achieved a Master's degree in Theatre. He was certainly an extraordinary teacher, and I am forever deeply grateful to him for the training I received in the countless years I spent studying in his studio. But I was never his devotee.

Susan wrote first to tell me that recently on two occasions, she and the entire class saw me there, fully embodied, though I was still in Europe! On the first occasion they saw me standing on O's front lawn. Then she claimed that they all saw me standing amongst them in O's studio. I re-read that section several times in disbelief. How could I be somewhere I wasn't? As foolish as that sounds, is as foolish as it struck me, though she claimed there were many witnesses. Toward the end of the letter, she seemed to be accusing me of failure at the Lab and wanted details. I burned the letter and sent her the ashes in response.

The following morning, I awoke in my little attic room with Jean asleep beside me. Then something very strange happened. I observed my hand and forearm lift off the bed though all of my body was still lying motionless upon the bed. It was as if another identical body existed within mine and was trying to lift itself out. I knew I was fully awake and not dreaming. I could not deny the bizarre experience, yet I had no idea what it was. I had never heard of "astral projection" but when I learned what it was, I came to believe that was what I had seen.

When Jean woke, I told him what had happened. He kindly did not suggest that I was going mad. We carried on with the day as if nothing unusual had happened.

Later that week Jean announced that he was going to Tunisia. Why? There was no answer. He responded to the question of when would he return with a shrug of his shoulders. But he told me I could use his motor scooter while he was away. I was surprised by his offer, while confused and saddened by the thought of his departure. However, he seemed determined. And I could not stop him.

So a few days after he was supposed to have left, I went to get the scooter from the inner yard of his grandmother's apartment building just down the street from where I lived. I found the key, hopped on, and took off.

At first it was fun, and it surprised me how easy it was to drive. Up Theophile Gautier, I sped. Carefree as could be, I paid little attention to where I was going. Bad choice. In moments I arrived at the Trocadero, a circle where twelve streets converge and cars were swerving around me in all directions. I was too panicked to hear the curses from drivers trying to avoid hitting me. By the time I reached the other side I was shaking and disoriented. I got off the scooter and walked it all the way home via the Tour Eiffel.

When I arrived in the alcove of Jean's building, there he was, standing as if waiting for me. I fell into his arms. Oh, those strong gentle arms. Why did my life have to take me from him, as we both knew one day it would.

"What happened to Tunisia?" I asked once I'd caught my breath.

"I didn't go," he said.

At the time, I assumed it was a matter of lack of funds. Now I realize he didn't want to leave me any more than I wanted to leave him. I could have made love to him right then and there, but instead we went back to my room.

*

Madame had her own idea of what would help me get through the disappointment that even she could feel. She asked me to come with them to their home in the Alps. They were expecting close family friends as guests. Anyway, I worked for her and she needed my help. I had been to Geneva once but never to the Alps. I was flown there once for a job interview that I thought was legitimate. But upon arrival at the not-such-a-gentleman's house, I quickly discovered he was looking for an assistant of another sort, and flew back to Paris the same day.

Madame's husband sat next to her on the train, silently reading the paper throughout the journey. It was almost as if he wasn't actually there. I sat across from Madame by the window and thoroughly enjoyed the ride down through the south of France, across northern Italy, and finally into the Southern Alps. Madame and I spoke only intermittently. We both liked the feeling of a train rolling along and the beautiful vistas that passed before our eyes. She had made wonderful tartines of Swiss cheese on thin slices of German pumpernickel, spread with butter for our lunch, and I gobbled them up.

When we arrived at their charming Swiss-style four-bedroom cabin, it was nearly buried in snow. Her groundskeeper met us there and shoveled a pathway to the front door. Once again, my sweet little bedroom could not have been more charming. Outside the pinewood-framed French window, the snow atop the mountain glistened like diamonds in the sun.

My duties for Madame on the trip were far fewer than at her home in Paris, so I had quite a bit of time to relax. I often sat on the balcony of a café watching the skiers speed down the slopes. Never having skied and unwilling to return to the States with a broken leg, I decided to stay off the slopes. Instead I strapped on snowshoes that look like tennis rackets and took long walks through the trees in the deep snow. I spent the evenings in a discotheque called L'Ouvre Boîte (The Open Box).

Dancing became my new thing. Perhaps I could dance my way back into light. Normally I danced alone and often the frenetic energy it created caused the crowd to form a circle around me, clapping with excitement, beckoning me on. Actually, it became a nightly experience. I enjoyed the attention of the Italians, who were there when we first arrived, and the French, who came when they left. Madame told me they purposely arranged their vacation times that way so as not to run into each other. "They don't like each other," she said.

Madame's guests had arrived with their 15-year-old son. He was a brilliant lad, who served to fill some of my time, especially at the dinner table, with the intellectual stimulus I needed. We discussed Rimbaud, among many other of my favorite poets, philosophers, and novelists.

It is possible that we may have appeared to be too enamored of one another. One night before leaving for the discotheque, I decided to give the lad one of my books on Rimbaud, Par Lui Meme (By Himself). I signed it, "Bonne chance dans l'etat d'homme" ("Good luck in the state of man"), as he was fond of discussing the "state of man."

I certainly saw no harm in this. Madame thought I was coming on to him and must have spent the night stewing over it, because very early in the morning she dragged me out of bed gruffly, demanding I shovel coal out of the cellar. Strange behavior for her, to say the least, not to mention that this was her husband's job. Yet there she stood over me, frothing at the bit. I was still half asleep, attempting to wield a heavy shovel against a pile of coal.

Just as I turned to pause a moment, she suddenly slapped me forcefully across the face. In my shocked expression she saw herself and apologized immediately. I was deeply humiliated to realize that I was in a position where she would even imagine she could strike me, as if I were her slave. My look of utter confusion must have made her realize that she was way off-track in her thinking. I saw in her face that she sincerely regretted her mistake. So I accepted her apology. "It's okay," I breathed. Instantly, I wished I had said it differently, as it was most certainly not okay, but I was willing to forgive her. We never discussed the matter again.

When we returned to Paris it was time to say my goodbyes. As far as I could see, I was getting nowhere in France. And though I loved Jean more than I yet knew, I felt my destiny awaited me.

One night, as a farewell of sorts, Jean and I got together with Eleanor and Emmanuelle and went to a discotheque called Club Set. It was primarily a hangout for the gay ballet boys. So just before we left my flat to go, I paused at the door saying to Jean, "Wait a minute." I reached in my purse for some lipstick and put it on Jean's lips. He allowed me without reproach and off we went.

We found the place easily and entered the very chic club. It was a bar unlike any I'd ever been in, where if you wanted a drink you had to buy the entire bottle, and it wasn't cheap. Also, wine was not available, so that meant buying a bottle of Grand Marnier or cognac. As I recall, we settled on cognac and I paid.

Then it was on to the dance floor and a free-for-all. I was wearing a vintage 1940s black crepe tunic-top dress with a full twirl skirt, trimmed in horizontal strips of black satin that hung just below my knees and above my favorite brown Earth Shoes. They were quite popular among the hippies of the day and comfortable enough to be the only shoes I'd brought with me to Europe.

I found myself slow dancing closely with a stranger, who whispered softly in my ear, "Are you a man or a woman?" I was surprised and amused by the question, uncertain what he'd hoped the answer would be. I told him the truth, nonetheless. As we stood in the lobby getting some air, he noticed my shoes, dropped to his knees, and embraced them.

"Oh my God, you are so adorable, I love them!"

Jean was somewhere enjoying a little uncensored fun, I imagine, as I didn't see him until we all left together.

Then came the heart-wrenching goodbyes, the train station, and the tears. Emmanuelle was there to take pictures of Jean and I that would come out like stills from a French film. Was it fair the way life kept moving along?

"I will come back, Jean. As soon as I can, I will come back."

"Yes, yes, sure, you will come back," he replied, in a tone heavy with disbelief. There was no way to convince him of what I couldn't be sure about myself.

We spent the last moments gazing deeply into one another's eyes, then looked away with long glances into empty distance and back again at each other. When it came time to board the train, tears fell like sheets of rain upon my face. But Jean, strong and brave, gently pushed me away, and waved au revoir.

Chapter Six — Grant

The simple kindness of friends is so helpful on the lone journeyer's way. My trip back to the States was seamlessly facilitated by a connection at Grot's theater. A friend gave me this young woman's name in New York City. I had called her from Paris, told her when I'd be arriving, and she just gave me her address and said, "Come. I'll do what I can to help you find a place."

I spent my first night in Brooklyn thanks to the kindness of a woman whose name I no longer remember. It was in one of those red brick buildings I still always see just before crossing the bridge into Manhattan. Turned out, it wasn't her apartment alone. She lived with her parents and they had been gracious enough to allow me, a complete stranger, to spend my first night back in the States on their living room sofa.

By morning I had a place to stay for as long as I liked. My hostess had actually done the research before I arrived and found one of her friends, Andy Potter, had a mattress on the floor of his living room just beneath his loft's edge.

Andy was ruggedly handsome, resembling what I suppose Paul Bunyan might have looked like, primarily because of his size. I wasn't the least bit attracted to him, which was probably a good thing.

The building was located at the very edge of the Lower East Side, just steps away from the corner of 1st Street and 2nd Avenue. The front steps were painted bright green. The interior hallways were grey. The apartment's front door opened into the kitchen, above which was the loft where Andy slept. To the left, overlooking the alleyway, was the bathroom. The kitchen was fairly large for New York apartments, and the living room was spacious enough for me to spread out my things comfortably.

Andy was very kind and considerate. He charged me minimal rent and told me I didn't need to pay him until I got a job, which I did almost immediately. I found work waitressing at a place called The Cookery in Washington Square. Famous jazz singers came there and sang standing beside the grand piano. I recall the food being good, wholesome, and sometimes great. I was only working three or four nights a week, and I had more than enough to survive in New York.

Andy seemed to know almost everyone in the theater world. He was an aspiring actor. I have no idea how talented he might have been. I spent my days checking out every corner of New York for a place where I could find actors to work with towards my goal of getting back to my ocean.

I audited a class of Richard Schechner at NYU, but I walked away without feeling much of a connection. I went on to a performance of Andre Gregory's "Manhattan Project". It was interesting but a little too highly stylized for my taste and not what I had in mind at all.

By chance however, one jewel rose up to greet me from Schechner's Performance Group. She was an actor named

Connie. I met her at one of those fabulous New York parties that only seem to happen in the city. Andy had been kind enough to tell me about it, inviting me to go along.

We entered through a door off the street, climbing up the narrow staircase to a grand loft fogged with the smoke of cigarettes and joints. It was crowded with actors, directors, producers, theatergoers, and film buffs anxious to enjoy, if possible, while getting as much as they could from being there. I, on the other hand, not at all a party girl, was amused by observing the antics of those around me, still keenly searching for my own kind.

Andy introduced me to Connie. She was a dark-haired, dark-eyed beauty, with a serious nature and a soft, deep, sultry voice. How could I not love her? The fact that I'd just come from Grotowski's Theater made me an instant celebrity and definitely aroused Connie's curiosity.

She regarded me intensely for several moments, then smiling brightly, she reached for the arm of a curly-haired young man standing nearby and introduced me to her guy Elliot. He was a fledgling film producer born into the industry as a descendent. They were making an independent short subject film they'd written together. It was intended to showcase Connie as an actress and Elliot as a director/producer. Connie suggested I visit them at their loft the next day. She wanted to hear the whole story of my work with Grot. I agreed to come and see them.

That following day we cemented our friendship. Their loft was a fairly large warehouse, artfully arranged into separate living spaces, as if rooms without walls. We spent a long afternoon together, the three of us sharing stories and languishing over a few joints as the sunlight poured through the large bare windows. Connie was sincerely interested in knowing what it had been like to work in the famous, highly revered Theatre Laboratorium.

She was extremely inquisitive and almost as intense as I was. She wanted every detail about the experience with Grot. I told her everything I could and perhaps more than I should, considering we were sworn to secrecy about the work. Many a pensive look would cross her face that day. Occasionally, she would speak softly aside, clearing in advance with Elliot what she was about to say or ask.

Interestingly enough, Connie began to share her own personal search, which she was working on with the famous trance researcher R.E.L. Masters. She suggested that perhaps I should consider working with him as well. "Perhaps there you might find what you seek."

"In trance?" I wondered. "Sure, why not? At this point I am willing to try almost anything!"

"Okay," Connie said, "I'll ask him if he's willing and get back to you. Meanwhile, Elliot and I have something we'd like to ask you." She glanced at Elliot for a reassuring nod and then looking into my eyes she said, "Elliot and I would like you to be in our movie."

I was taken aback. Wasn't it clear that I had no further interest in acting? She seemed momentarily perplexed by my hesitation. Had they imagined that I would jump at the chance? Still, I was intrigued and agreed to do it. They were both quite pleased, saying they'd fill me in later.

Within a few days, Connie called to tell me that Masters was in fact interested in working with me. It was a rainy morning when his assistant Veronica came to take me on an hour's drive into the country for my first meeting with Masters. We arrived at the home of Burgess Meredith, hidden away in the forests of Pomona, New York. Robert Masters was leasing the property with his wife Jean. Bob, as she called him, was still sleeping.

I paced the kitchen for a while, then ventured into the living room. It was filled with ancient Egyptian artifacts, including two upright mummy cases, gorgeously carved and painted, complete with death masks and robes. I immediately assumed this was Masters' collection, when suddenly he was standing behind me assuring me it was not. It was, in fact, Meredith's.

"Huh," I thought, "wouldn't have guessed it."

Bob properly introduced himself, shaking my hand, and led me on a guided tour through the rather large house and grounds. I was fascinated by the wealth of collected relics from ancient mythology, yet I was anxious to begin the work.

Masters suggested we start the day with some yoga exercises. We worked on some basic stretches for about an hour and then had lunch prepared by his assistant. He asked me to give him a brief history of my life, what I was looking for and why I had come to him.

I explained that after comparing notes with Connie, I thought he might know something about this wild frontier I so desperately sought to recapture, the ocean of fire, the sea of light. He made no comment that indicated he knew what I was talking about. Doesn't mean he didn't.

We decided to begin our first attempt at an induced trance. Masters asked me to lay stretched out on the floor and relax my entire body as he gave suggestions. "Slowly your eyelids will become too heavy to remain open, and when they close, you will see warm colors of red, green, blue, and yellow." My eyes persistently remained open.

Bob switched to a different instruction. "Imagine you have a journal in your hands, open to two blank pages. Now write your name on one page and 'trance' on the other. Be careful to note the texture of the paper, the smell of the ink, and the sound while writing, consciously forming each letter."

I completed this task successfully while Masters counted backwards from one thousand. Soon I could not decipher if my eyes were opened or closed, as a blinding white light washed over my vision.

Bob repeated the suggestion of deep colors flashing across my eyes, but I was seeing pastels like watercolors of blue, pink, yellow, and lavender.

Then I began to experience an increasing pressure on the back of my head, which I attributed to the sharpness of the plush carpet I was lying on.

When I could no longer bear it, I asked, "Is this a particularly sharp carpet? Because if feels as if my head is on a bed of razors!"

Masters assured me that it was not.

I ventured further, "Is it normal to experience an incredible amount of pain in this process?"

He again assured me that it was not. "Though in some isolated cases," he said, "the first attempts are more agonizing than others, but it does not necessarily mean the work is futile."

"I believe you," I said. At that point I realized that if nothing else had been accomplished, I had begun to trust him.

We did not go further that first day but promised to meet again soon. It was not at all unusual for me to meet with tremendous resistance whenever any work called for me to go beyond myself. To overcome these barriers, I often incurred a considerable amount of physical pain.

Two weeks later I returned to Masters' home late in the afternoon. Anxious for this meeting's success, and finding him hopeful, I was ready to work.

He instructed me to sit back in an easy chair and concentrate on a strobe light flashing on the ceiling. He tried the same light directly against my forehead as well, eyes shut. I explained to him that though engulfed in the flashing white lights, I saw no colors and was disheartened despite the interesting effects. Only now do I realize how little colors mattered, so why set up expectations for the unimaginable?

I think it was Dick Sutphen who wrote that those who attended the ancient Egyptian Mystery School were given a block against hypnosis for that life and any subsequent lifetime in order to protect their secrets. Seemed Bob was trying to get me to put myself into a trance, as all attempts to accomplish this were failing. He tried the sound of a metronome, which I heard as drops of water falling like Chinese water torture. I passed through that imagery and allowed the sound to drop painlessly on my center, each beat increasing my concentration. I enjoyed the sound immensely. I wanted to go with its simplicity, though I felt myself resisting its call.

It was from this level of consciousness that Masters began suggesting situations for the awakening of visual imagery on a journey through several rooms.

"You are about to enter a room that is filled with clothes. Explore the contents of the room, touch the fabrics. You may try on anything you like."

I saw myself enter what appeared to be a good-sized

room in an attic, much like the one in my first childhood home. The walls were painted faded green. An old grey carpet covered the floor. There was a large armoire with mirrored doors at one end of the room, and antique trunks were scattered throughout. Clothes were strewn everywhere, bursting out of the trunks or lying in heaps on the floor. There was a musty attic smell that was depressing from the outset. I looked at the garments that appeared to be from every period of history for something appealing to try on.

I took a long, white chiffon evening gown, styled in a Greek fashion, and admired its free-flowing movement in twirls in front of the closet mirror. There was a costume from the Elizabethan Age in green brocade. It was difficult to get into, though it had a rather stately, regal effect. It seemed that everything I had ever dreamed of wearing was there and no longer needed.

I began to look for something else, and searching through the trunks I came upon a hair shirt, tucked away in the bottom of a trunk beneath many layers of paraphernalia. I stripped myself naked and put it on. It was a greyish-brown color, and I soon found a rope to tie around my waist. The preliminary itching turned to a subtle burning, and my skin began to turn red, but there was something comforting about the way I looked in it. I thought of John the Baptist, the locust and the desert.

Lastly, I caught sight of a Mercy Nun's habit. It took time and effort to put it on properly but when I did, I felt its restrictions in the greatest detail. Every nun that ever taught me flashed quickly in my mind. I understood why they were constantly fidgeting with the headpiece and the bib, as it was cumbersome and tight around the face. Despite its holy appearance, it was a bit too romantic for me, and I began to sweat. I wanted to leave the room, so I changed back into the original jeans and shirt I was wearing in the session and waited instruction to enter the next room.

Masters spoke again: "You are about to enter a large banquet room where there is a full-sized banquet table, upon which has been laid a great feast. I want you to go to the table and feel free to taste anything you wish."

It strikes me how the slightest suggestion in that trance state unfurls so rapidly, taking on a life of its own. With some resistance as I was not hungry, I entered the banquet hall. The walls and floor were mahogany. The banquet table was complete with candelabras surrounded by grapes and a buffet fit for a king. I took a drumstick in one hand—delicious, crisp, and juicy—and a glass of 1959 vintage Bordeaux in the other. I tasted melons, cantaloupes, steaks, and Polish vodka. As I continued around the table, the foods became simpler: hors-d'oeuvres of chopped liver and unleavened bread.

At this point the entire scene changed. The elaborate feast disappeared.

The table was suddenly set before immense arched windows of the same length. Only the unleavened bread remained with simple goblets of wine. I was re-approaching the table, surrounded by guests from a different angle now.

I recognized that the guests represented the various apostles and Christ Himself. Each apostle bore the visage of a different man I had known in my life. It was the Last Supper.

I focused a few seconds on the face of Judas as I walked around the table to stand behind the Christ. The others were unaware of my presence, though I was certain He was aware of me. I stood almost frozen, as though intently waiting for something. Then He turned around and looked into my face. As with the others, His face was not unknown to me; it was Grotowski.

In a moment, he turned back to the others, pushed his chair back and got up, seemingly excusing himself from the table. He walked out into the garden dressed in a white hooded gown. I did not see his face again, but followed just a step behind him. He led me in silence down a wide forest path. The soil was dry and rocky, though the trees were lush. At the end of this path the sun was hanging like an enormous ball of yellow fire over a steep cliff. When we reached the edge, he disappeared.

Then Masters gave a new suggestion: "Before you there are three holes. At the bottom of one is water, of another is wind, and of the other is fire. I want you to descend into each of these. You may choose the order in which you enter, but you must enter each."

I found myself in the great hall of what appeared to be a medieval castle. In the distance there were stone archways and a staircase. The walls and floor of the chamber were also stone. Before me there were three massive wells in a row, the walls hewn of large rocks. The atmosphere was dimly lit, silent, almost lonely, were it not for the elements awaiting me.

I chose the well of water as my first meeting, descending the spiral staircase along the inside wall. At the base of the stairs there was a pool of calm, dark water that cast no reflection. The smell of the algae and moss on the stones was sweet. I entered the water slowly, swimming freely. The cool stream fell in crystals from my fingertips, a baptism of sorts. After this refreshing interlude, I mounted the staircase and prepared to enter the next well.

I descended into the well of wind on a staircase similar to the first, but just before reaching the midway point, I was swept up by the outer skirts of the tornado within. Like a child unafraid of crashing into the walls, I felt myself being pulled into the center with tremendous force, hurled wildly about and cast downwards in a spiraling motion until I was approaching the very heart of a frenzied abyss. Then suddenly I shot like a rocket up through the cylindrical void of winds all around and landed safely again on the great stone floor.

Now it was time, and there could be no more delay, to enter the well of fire. I felt a terribly dark fear wash over me as I approached its outer rim. Overly concerned and preoccupied with symbolic imagery since the very word fire was introduced, I tried to excuse myself from entering the fire.

But Masters encouraged me with kindness, and so I began to descend gingerly down the stone steps lit by a great wall of flames. The steps were scalding hot. My flesh was already reddened and blistering by the time I reached the bottom platform. All that was left now was the jump, so I gave myself up, with Masters calling in the distance, "Burn, burn."

I don't know if it was the words themselves or more likely the assurance of another's presence that gave me the courage. I was completely immersed in the flames that held me amongst them. There was an indescribable joy as my body was burned away. Flesh, charred to the skeleton, dissolved as I became the fire. Then my being looked upwards and I saw my flames licking the blue sky, surrounded by a forest that held my furnace in its clearing. Amidst the flames redoubling and multiplying, I drew back, and recollecting my human form, I stood again in safety on the chamber floor.

The next was to be the last room. "You are entering a large empty room with a wooden floor." I was relieved and anxious at the same moment. Relieved because I so love this type of room and anxious because I knew it was time to begin my real work.

I started from a squatting position like a frog leaping high into the air as I circled the room. Mid-air in a leap, I became a bird. Flapping my arms wildly, they took on the appearance of great wings. The feathers were just about to burst into the flames of a firebird when I collapsed in exhaustion on the floor. The visual imagery section of this session ended.

The next morning, I woke feeling completely refreshed, rejoicing in sunlight upon the grass. I sat with Masters a while as he asked about the things that are often deeply hidden, and I was surprised by my candid responses. I was grateful for the opportunity to sincerely express certain ideas and feelings that were concrete to my existence without shame or fear of being thought ridiculous. It was as though our discussion was revealing a burden that I was unaware of carrying, and by so doing, lightened it.

In our work together we had tried everything, including a witch's cradle. I told him, "I understand more clearly now the importance of the place as it relates to the search, the variable being who is searching, and specifically for what.

Trance or a hypnotic state guided by suggestion doesn't seem to work for me, perhaps because the words in and of themselves do not have any real meaning for me and are not essential."

Sometime later I realized that the principal difference between our works was that in mine, if you shut your eyes, you'll miss it! I began to consider returning to O to get back to the sea.

Late that day I left Masters' home, never to return. There was something calling me from the empty room with the wooden floors. I kissed both of Bob's hands and ran out into the yard, a little heavy-hearted and absolutely empty-eyed.

Connie was, of course, highly curious about the details of my time with Robert Masters. I did have the impression she was enamored of him, at least somewhat. But I would never have guessed what I would discover googling him decades later, that his research was primarily focused on sexual discovery through trance. I guess Kate's casual comment to me once that I am myopic was, at times, not far off.

I wonder if I frustrated him? And I wonder, even more now, the reason for Connie's intense interest? Ah well, she and Elliot were about ready to start filming their short and I had yet to see the script. When I asked what she'd like me to wear for the shoot, she said, "Anything you like."

I decided on an Yves St. Laurent dress I found in a magazine. It was off one shoulder like a Grecian robe in flowing chiffon. Connie knew a seamstress in the garment district who specialized in airbrush fabric painting. I took her the picture of the dress and told her I wanted her to paint birds in flight from a forest on fire. The dress turned out so beautifully that I have kept and worn it on special occasions throughout the years. I am not so sure Connie was pleased with the final product, as it may have turned out to be a bit upstaging!

In truth, I did upstage her on the set that day as we filmed on the pier. At one point, I walked ahead of Connie, blocking her from the camera's view. It was entirely unintentional, but it clearly annoyed her. I wasn't needed for the second day of shooting and left New York before the project was finished. It would be two decades before I finally got a copy of it from Elliot.

Meanwhile, I had invited Chloe and Emmanuelle to come for a visit so I could show them America. Emmanuelle alone accepted my invitation. I had made up my mind to return to work, but first I wanted to see the northern states, having seen the southern states as a child. Soon after Emmanuelle arrived, we took off on our adventure in a Greyhound bus.

I used my considerable skills in tour planning to create a wonderful trip. Emmanuelle was very laid back and so easy to be with. She was journaling all along the way. At times it did annoy me a little, because she seemed to write as if she was painting a portrait. She would look up at me and then scribble something down. I suppose I thought she was writing about me. It made me feel somewhat scrutinized. Other than that, it was a pleasant journey together. We were young and entirely free. We could do whatever we wanted. And now, we chose to see America. I am a true patriot. Always have been.

*

Though our destination was ultimately Ossetynski's Actors Laboratory in Hollywood, we would be making a stopover at my first love's house in Aptos. Spark was waiting for us. He had only recently married the first of his three wives. Lena was a petite young Philippine woman. I met her just briefly once. She was a student and opted to spend the weekend at her mother's when Spark announced that we were coming.

He had a tiny little house on the edge of a creek with a small backyard. Spark was all smiles and welcoming when we arrived. He and Emmanuelle got on well from the start.

As I dropped my bags in his house, I breathed a heavy sigh of relief. I was almost home at last, and Spark's place was near enough for now. I was anxious to share my extraordinary experience with him. He was, as always, interested in anything that might broaden his scope of knowledge, and so he listened intently to my story. I doubt that it really landed for him at that time, though many years later he would inquire about it again.

Spark offered us some of the LSD he was taking but we both declined. We all hung out together smoking hash and cigarettes, sharing stories and having fun. As Spark was coming on to the acid, he informed us that after years of practicing some yoga bends, "I am now able to suck my own cock." And as if just the thought of it was not enough, he then proved it to us by actually giving a full demonstration! I was a little worried that my friend might be uncomfortable if not shocked by Spark's behavior. Turned out I was the prude. Her feathers were not at all ruffled. In fact, she was quite amused. I did wonder quietly to myself where his tiny wife put all that.

Spark loved adventure and goading others into joining him. His dares had often helped me to go beyond what I thought I could do. I rarely back down from a challenge. Spark suggested we head down to the shore and baptize ourselves in the cold ocean.

"Wonderful!" I said.

"Great idea!" Emmanuelle agreed.

I remember we walked in the dark of night down the narrow winding path that led to the sea. Once on the beach, Spark and Emmanuelle quickly shed their clothes, dropping them on the shore, and leapt into the cold ocean. I was reluctant but eventually followed suit and jumped in with them.

Once back at the house, there was a profound interaction between Emmanuelle and me. Standing too close and staring deep into my eyes, she asked, "Can you never just be in the moment?"

Something about the idea of being in the moment almost terrified me. What was it about being present that made me so uncomfortable? Worse, she must have noticed that I was rarely there in those days or she would not have been asking, hence my doubled discomfort. She was too kind to press the point much further, but it struck me in a way that I have never forgotten her question or that moment.

Spark had arranged for us to stay in a small cabin owned by an acupuncturist friend of his. There were two goats in the yard. We planned to stay about a week.

Emmanuelle and Spark took classes in the ancient Indian Kathakali Dance for several hours each day. I had been studying that for several years already in O's class, taught by Yarosha. So I chose to stay behind to write and reflect. I wasn't interested in engaging in more exercises just for the sake of doing something. I was clear what my goal was. Anything that was not able to take me closer to that goal was not of interest to me nor worth my time.

Lately, Spark had been dabbling in black magic with his close friend Pete. He was living with Pete in Claremont when I found their house that night, so stoned on mescaline that it's a miracle I made it there alive.

Pete was a fairly tall, dark-haired, husky man of Polish descent. By odd coincidence, when I was fourteen, I had sung Gounod's "Ave Maria" for Pete's wedding at the request of Father Patrick. Spark would meet Pete sometime later, shortly before his divorce from what turned out to be a short-lived marriage.

Pete had achieved three PhDs: one in Theology, one in Philosophy, and one in Ancient Religions. He also taught at Kate's high school, and so our mutual lover Lorin had known him as well. I would never have met him were it not for the close friendship that ensued between him and Spark. They were obsessed with Paganism. Spark wanted to understand, revisiting the pre-Christian era by experiencing it. Pete gathered together their friends who were also believers and created a coven of thirteen.

When the moon was nearing its fullness, Spark pleaded with Pete to allow Emmanuelle and me to join in their full moon ritual. Until then he had enforced a rule: no girls in the coven. Pete finally acquiesced, and we were invited to join that night.

They had built a stone altar in the backyard of Pete's Aptos home. When night fell and the moon rose in the sky, shedding its glimmering light everywhere, a fire was lit on the altar, and we all gathered around in a circle. Once the circle was created, they began to evoke the spirits, chanting "Satana, Lucifer" and then "Beelzebub" (also known as the Lord of the Flies) and it was the mention of that particular name that signaled me it was time to leave.

I had no hesitation but just before breaking the circle, I crossed over to Pete, and much to my own shock and disbelief, bent down to the ground and kissed his feet! Then I walked away as swiftly as possible and sought refuge in the lobby of the old Aptos Inn nearby.

Looking back, it somehow reminds me of a moment in Dostoyevsky's Brothers Karamazov. All three brothers: Ivan the intellectual, Dmitri the debauchee, and Alyosha the holy one are standing with Alyosha's mentor, the saintly monk. Suddenly, solemnly, the old monk stands, crosses the room, and bending down to the ground, kisses the feet of Dmitri! Everyone there was stunned except for Dmitri, who was humbled and perhaps forever changed by it.

By the time I went back to retrieve Emmanuelle, everyone still there was very drunk. Spark and Emmanuelle were nowhere to be found. Pete approached me, poured me a glass of wine, and took me to his bed. I went willingly. I made love to him, going down on him, and enjoyed how empowered his ecstasy made me feel. He wasn't able to do much for me, though his tenderness was enough expression of his gratitude.

We fell asleep and then woke in the barest light of dawn with flies landing on us as if we were turds on the ground. No amount of waving off dissuaded them. It was truly disturbing and gave me one of the clearest indications I can remember of having done something wrong. I felt ashamed. I never told Spark, and I am quite certain Pete didn't either, because I would surely have heard about it.

I went back to our cabin, where Spark and Emmanuelle were waiting for me. Spark told me that Pete and his boys were all outraged by my behavior. By breaking the circle, he explained, "You opened us up to psychic attacks from the spirit world, where we were negotiating our way." Emmanuelle had stayed and evidently conducted herself appropriately. "Everyone enjoyed her presence," he said.

I remained silent. Nothing he could say would have made me regret leaving when I did. It would be a long time before I would actually explain to Spark why I had left. Besides, I don't live in fear of others' opinions of me and my behavior. No judge was harsher than the one within me whom I was struggling to unseat!

Some years later, Spark wrote to tell me Pete had killed himself; "At the spring equinox ceremony, a week before he committed suicide, Pete had us all sit in a circle and went around it with a basin washing everyone's feet." He was not the first of those who had touched my life to commit suicide, and to my great sadness, far from the last.

Soon it was time to go back home. There was no more delaying it. The force of my life continued to drive me onward. On the morning of our departure, we gathered up our things, and each of us threw our arms around Spark—hugging, kissing, and thanking him for his many kindnesses. He stopped me for just a moment and looked deeply in my eyes. I almost cried. I have never liked leaving him, yet I was never able to stay.

We headed south on our last Greyhound bus ride. Within hours we were dragging our bags up the stairs to Susan's place in Hollywood just above O's apartment. We dropped our bags in Susan's flat. She hugged and kissed me, then pulling back, looked into my eyes as if searching for an answer, which she would not have understood anyway.

I introduced Emmanuelle, and then Susan kindly showed us to the beds she'd arranged for us to stay on as long as we liked. We dropped our things and headed down to see Ossetynski.

After giving me a cursory embrace, he greeted Emmanuelle in a gentlemanly manner, almost flirting with her. Then taking me privately into his kitchen, motioning to the table where I'd last seen him sit with Grotowski, he sat across from me and began his cross examination.

"So what happened?" he asked in his deep penetrating voice. I told him of my extraordinary experience in Grot's theater. When I finished my detailed story, he looked at me crossly. "I don't believe you!" he blurted out as if shouting. "If this had really happened to you, Grotowski would not have sent you away!"

I was surprised by his disbelief. First of all, how would anyone be able to make up such an experience? How could he not know the difference between the truth and a lie, especially when told by his most beloved student?

But then I considered another possibility. How could I have experienced something that had evaded him these many years of his life? It was either that or he simply had some misconception about what exactly they were doing in The Theater Laboratory, that it was not a matter of individual achievement; it was primarily a collaboration. And then, who did you want to work with? Who would fit in the ensemble? And my ability to work in an ensemble was limited at best and would always remain so.

O agreed to allow me back in his class, which was all that I needed at the time. His personal approval had never meant much to me and even less now that I had an entirely private goal. Still his guidance as my teacher and his opinion of my work as an artist continued to have some meaning for me.

*

Within a few days, I went to see my parents in their home. My father wrapped his arms around me and held me tightly for a moment. He was grateful to have his prodigal daughter returned. Mother barely acknowledged me, blatantly giving me the silent treatment. It must have been from her that I learned how to treat those who in my estimation crossed some line that rendered them dead for me. I could easily stand in the same room with someone, totally disavowing their existence, as if in the place they stood there was nothing at all. I know how disturbing it is to be treated like this, and it is the worst punishment I am capable of delivering to anyone.

I figured in my ridiculous arrogance that she was probably jealous because I had dared to do what I wanted, whereas she was tied down to a life that left her little liberty. Was it really this? Or was it because in all my time away, I wrote almost exclusively to my father and not to her?

Even as a very young child I remember her expressing some resentment about how little I was willing to share with her. Perhaps I was afraid if I got too close to her, I would become like her—trapped. The one thing we always had in common was our love of cooking, and only in the kitchen did I feel close to her. From her I learned all the basics, and there are still a few dishes of hers I can't quite seem to duplicate. They are missing her essence, as do I now.

I have always enjoyed cooking dishes from around the world, much to the delight of my family and friends. My palette is discerning enough for me to recreate almost anything I have tasted.

Eventually Mother began speaking to me again. We never discussed it. Years later she let me know how proud she was of me. And I would one day know how hard she had tried to protect me.

*

I decided to stay in L.A. for a while. I guess I needed a break from the intense closeness of constant traveling with Emmanuelle. So she stayed with Susan while I stayed in a lovely little two-bedroom Beverly Hills apartment of a young couple away on a month's vacation who said I was welcome to stay in the spare bedroom until they returned. I told them I'd be looking for my own flat and would stay only until then. I had an unusual way of finding places to live in those days. I would decide where I wanted to live and then negotiate to get it.

This time it was Yarosha's old place off Beachwood Drive in Hollywood, in the charming canyon neighborhood just under the famous Hollywood sign. I went to see the old gentleman who owned the flat. It was part of his large Spanish-style home on Glen Holly. The house had been split into several apartments. The one I wanted was entered by the rustic, dark wood front door of the lovely grand house. The entryway displayed a large, stained glass window and there was a substantial storage closet on that level as well. A staircase made of terra cotta tiles led up to the wonderful large single room with great French windows, opening like large doors over an ivy-bordered garden staircase that led up the side of the house. The room was small, though complete, with a Murphy bed, a large walk-in closet, a white ceramic tiled bathroom with a full-length mirror on the outside of the door, and a tiny separate corner kitchen with louvered windows on two sides.

The gentle old man was quite surprised when I knocked on his door asking if I could have the apartment. I explained that I was a friend of Yarosha's and knew of the place from him. After looking me over and considering for a moment, he said the current tenant was in arrears and he would give her notice and have it available for me in two weeks! I was leaping for joy down the street, not the least bit sorry for the person losing her place to me. Just then I bumped into an actor friend named David, who had briefly studied with us in O's studio. It had been much too challenging for him. He remembered me and asked if I'd like to go to a party that night. I said sure and took the address saying I'd see him there.

It was a pleasant enough party, though I hadn't intended to stay long. I noticed a petite thin woman, with a beautifully chiseled face, long blonde straight hair, and a somewhat flat chest.

David came up to me and said, "There is someone who wants to meet you." Sure enough, it was the lovely little blonde.

"My name is Lee," she said, as I took her hand.

"She wants to go out with you," David said in front of her, and she didn't blush.

I considered for just a moment and said, "Give me your number, and I'll give you a call." I had never made love to a woman, and after giving it a little more thought, I decided to give her call and take her out. She was very pleased to hear from me. I suggested we meet in the dining room of the Rainbow Bar and Grill.

We met there that same night. She was charming and beautiful. We got to know each other a little over a delicious dinner. Then she asked if she could come home with me. That was, after all, what I was there for, and so I said yes. I didn't tell her I'd never really made love to a woman before. I wanted to know if I could.

She was anxious and more than willing. I saw no harm in experimenting with her. I hoped I wouldn't disappoint her. I was still staying in Beverly Hills at the time. We kissed a little in the living room, then excusing ourselves, we slipped into the bathroom one by one to wash up.

How few men ever bother to do that? What makes them think shaking the pee off their penises is sufficient cleansing before hopping into bed hoping to have it sucked off?

When I entered the bedroom, she was already in the bed naked and only partially covered to the waist. I stopped a moment admiring her loveliness and the soft lust washing over her face as I disrobed and her nipples hardened. Gently I drew the sheet from her body and gingerly climbed in, wrapping her in my arms. What a rush of warmth poured through my body. I immediately understood why some men loved breasts so much! They are so soft and comforting. I kissed her neck, then across both shoulders, and down to her sweet breasts that I caressed, kissed, and sucked gently.

Lee was delighted, so responsive. She directed me with the lightest touch on my shoulders as she opened her legs wide. I found my way to her mound, licking her as she began to moan. She grasped my hair as I sucked her clitoris and let my tongue reach up into her, darting in and out, licking all around until she was screaming in ecstasy. I held her in my arms encouraging her to enjoy the glow and gently declined her reciprocating. I was left with the feeling that this is how an impotent man must feel, unable to respond.

*

Emmanuelle and Susan were getting along well, and so she continued to stay with Susan as I moved into my new place. I also very quickly found a job waitressing at place called "Simply Blues". It was located at Sunset and Vine on the top floor of a twenty story corporate tower.

I quickly became the favorite waitress of the customers and owners as well. However, with the owners, it would be short-lived.

One day, while making what I thought would be a quick stop, I parked in a red zone. When I came out, not only was a cop writing me a ticket, he was having my car towed away! Apparently, I had several unpaid parking tickets that had gone to warrant. The next thing I knew he took my purse, cuffed me, and put me in the back of his squad car. I knew I was in more trouble than he thought, because there was a small bag of pot in my purse.

Once in the station, I was stripped and cavity-searched by big Bertha, who commented to the officer later, "She's clean, really clean." How disgusting! The officer had found the bag and worse, a pain pill that an elderly woman customer had given me for shoulder pain I had complained about. I have never liked pills and I hadn't taken it. I was told that possession of that particular pill was a felony.

Then I was given my one phone call, and I called Shelly, the woman whose apartment I was just recently staying in. Perhaps I chose to call her because the bail was about

$5,000, and she was the only one I thought might have it. I was placed in a holding cell like a birdcage, alone thank God, until Shelly arrived with the bail. She had put her gorgeous diamond ring up as a guarantee.

Happily, I had made friends with a customer at work, Ron Cohen. He was a kind reputable lawyer, and when I told him what had happened, he took my case pro bono. It was this type of kindness I would learn to pay forward to others. He got me off with a misdemeanor that would be erased from my record in seven years, and I would have to attend diversion classes to be completed some months later. The single pill felony charge was dropped. I lost touch with Shelly not long after; she moved out of state. A friendship lost or misplaced, I have always regretted missing.

It wasn't long before I received a call from Lee, inviting me to dinner at her home with her husband. Evidently, they had an open marriage. I was intrigued and agreed to come. They had a charming duplex on Hollywood's west side.

Lee was a gracious hostess and had prepared a delicious meal. Her husband was an attractive young man, though quiet. I hadn't yet guessed what they were planning until after dinner when Lee led me into their bedroom to show me their four-poster bed. And then she seductively began removing her clothes while her husband sat on a chair in the background.

I stood frozen watching her as I began to feel my excitement rise. When she got down to her bra and panties, she strolled up and began undressing me until I stood completely naked before them both. She ran her hands across my shoulders and gently over my breasts. Then she removed her bra and panties, and grasping my hands, tugged me onto the bed. I was burning with excitement now and began to make love to her while her husband watched. Then suddenly he was on the bed as well, entering me from behind as I sucked her off, and we all came together in a wildly erotic moment.

The next day in the supermarket I wondered if anyone could tell I'd been with a woman. It struck me as a strange thought, but was I gay? More likely, according to my sexual history, I was bisexual. But I asked myself, could I be in a relationship with a woman? No, I did not believe I could deal with the emotions of a woman. I struggled enough with my own. And besides, I enjoyed the completion I felt with a man. Not to mention the competition that always seemed to exist in relations with men, which I enjoyed and was good at.

Sometime too soon after that, I looked into a mirror and saw, to my absolute horror, the Bell's Palsy had returned again. I was devastated. I called Lee quietly weeping and told her I could not see her again.

Sexual escapades aside, I continued to be committed to my primary goal, the discovery of a way back into the eternal essence of that energy, too little known. I had started back in O's class, and Emmanuelle joined us for a time as well. The work was as grueling as ever. I was trying to maintain a normal life despite my paralysis having returned.

I tried to continue on at my job until the owner gruffly took me aside, rudely saying he couldn't have me gurn at his customers and fired me on the spot. I've come to notice that people who dare to treat me with such outrageous cruelty usually don't fare well for long. His restaurant burned down sometime later in a tragic event very reminiscent of a film called The Towering Inferno. Albeit his tower was a bit shorter. Of course, I had nothing to do with it, but it was interesting.

Back in O's studio, which he was now calling "The Ossetynski Actors Laboratory," I began working on what would be the equivalent of my Master's thesis.

O's plan was to take us all to Poland and show his work in the Institute Kultura and for me to perform it there. It was the Cultural Institute of Poland, regarded as the top performance hall in all of Warsaw.

My love of the Belgian poet Rimbaud led me to use his Season in Hell as the basis of my solo performance that would serve as my Master's thesis. I played three characters within that one piece. One was the young soldier, modeled after Stavrogin in Camus' The Possessed using Rimbaud's text. Then there was the foolish virgin, as Rimbaud titled the second section; and lastly, the androgynous. It took a long time and a lot of work to edit it down to a performable piece without losing its essence. I alternated between the French text and an excellent English translation done by Wallace Fowlie. The piece lent itself well to that format. I wanted to show the range of my capabilities before I left theater forever. I would struggle with the piece for over a year before performing it in Warsaw.

Meanwhile, when class ended at 10 pm, I stayed on after everyone left and attempted to throw myself back into light, hurling myself through the air, leaping up and down attempting to duplicate the movements that had once taken me there. Night after night I returned home again in despair. Never once did I suppose I had merely imagined it. It was the most real, actual, concrete experience of my life until then, and I would find it again or die trying!

One Sunday morning, O walked through the door with a handsome young man named Grant. He proudly introduced him as a student of Grotowski who had made "Holiday" with Grot in the south of France.

Grant was a tall, well-built brunette, but I felt no sexual attraction to him, possibly because he was gay and in a committed relationship. I was interested in hearing everything he was willing to tell me about his work with Grot, already surmising that he must have worked with Chloe in that same "Holiday".

We went out for coffee after class to share our experiences with the work, despite both of us having been cautioned not to discuss the work outside. Lucky for me, in this case, I simply assumed that he, like Chloe, had burned in "Holiday". I would not find out until it no longer mattered that he had no such experience.

I rambled on about the great genius of Grot until he finally stopped me to say, "If you think Grotowski is so great, you should meet my Teacher because he makes Grotowski look like an ant!" Now he had my full attention. He said that this Teacher had shown him how to go within, inside himself and experience a magnificent peace.

Chapter Seven — The Gift

I felt as if I had turned over every rock on earth and searched the world seeking the ocean of joy.

As a student I had to pin my eyelids open to finish reading Siddhartha. Having freed myself from Catholicism by the age of twelve, anything that smacked of religion, let alone Eastern mysticism, repelled me. Still I could not leave this stone unturned.

Having taken all the pertinent information from Grant, I found my way to the venue. It was a beautiful hall, entered through double doors. A wide, steep staircase led up to the large hall. I climbed up, skipping every other step. Mahogany benches lined the walls, and rows of chairs were in the center, all nearly filled. Entering a room full of strangers had been very difficult for me as a child, but now I was trained to take up lots of space that kept the fear away.

I found a seat at the front quickly. I have never really understood why those are the seats usually left open until last. Lucky for me, I only wanted to sit there, except when I thought there was a chance I'd want to leave early, in which case I would sit in back. But here I was determined to discover what, if anything, this Teacher could show me. What was he offering? And was there any chance it was the way back?

On this particular night, they showed a video of him speaking. If I had not seen and heard him, it is quite possible I would never have returned. When the film began, a boy spoke, whose voice was still changing, periodically cracking and squeaking. No matter, because I quickly became intrigued by what he was saying and his delivery.

I thought to myself, "Well, if nothing else, he is a great actor," because the slightest movement of his hand was entirely captivating. He spoke of a profound peace that could be found within oneself. He said that he could show someone how to find it. Then he said something of critical importance to me, "The reason that I cannot charge you for this is because I am not taking something out of my pocket and giving it to you. I am taking something out of your pocket and showing it to you!"

Now he had me. That it should be free was a primary stipulation for me. Once I took MDA (a psychedelic) alone. I went wandering through Wattles Glen, a hidden wild garden maintained by Buddhist monks. As I came onto the drug, I was filled with an intensely peaceful feeling. All at once I realized that there was no need to hurry anywhere. I was breathing, and the air itself was alive and full of beauty.

It was almost enough for me. But in the next moment I was filled with anger and resentment. Logically, I knew it was impossible for a drug to provide any experience that didn't already exist within me. I cried out to God, "Please, I beg you, let me find the missing piece that will make my life complete. And if I have to take some drug or pay for it, I do not want it, nor do I want this life without it!"

So there sat the young Teacher speaking of a primordial vibration, a sweetness, an energy so beautiful, he said, 'If you took all the trees and made them into paper and all the oceans and turned them into ink, you could not describe the beauty of this gift.'

There was something about his flowery yet descriptive speech that rang true in my heart. Something I was familiar with, something I knew, beckoning me from within. I was determined to receive this gift he was so freely offering. With a joy yet foreign to me, I was told that all I had to do was come and listen until I was sure I wanted this gift, then when a representative came to town, I could ask to receive it.

"How soon would that be?" I asked.

Someone would be coming in two weeks, they said.

Two weeks, I thought, I can do this.

And I did. I went every night for the next two weeks. I didn't dare miss once. I was in earnest to discover what he might be hiding in this gift, that one could only receive if they truly wanted it.

I listened to one person after another speaking from their hearts about some profound experience that seemed to embody attributes of the awesome experience I had in Poland. One of the many other things that struck me was the variety in the group itself which was comprised of doctors, lawyers, engineers, actors, musicians, professors, and yes, plenty of hippies. Not only did it strike me as an unlikely gathering of so many dissimilar people, but that I would find myself sitting among them was quite incredible as well.

I was concerned about the perfection within, so often spoken of by those attempting to describe their experience while practicing this gift. If it was true that perfection existed within, how could I go on creating in the face of it?

At the same time, I was especially taken seeing the children running up and down the aisles without reprimand. They seemed to be happy. Their parents were evidently elevated enough to stay off their backs. I thought to myself, I should probably do this, if only for the sake of my future children. I tried to use logic as I continued to access the information that was being shared. I wanted to understand and at the same time I knew that only receiving the gift could prove to me there was any connection in reality to what I had already experienced.

The two weeks passed quickly, and I was relieved to think that I would soon have the evidence to prove whether or not the Teacher's promise was true and my question would be answered. I needed proof, absolute irrefutable proof. The representative arrived and was meeting with people at the hall. He was a man from India, dressed in a white kurta and dhoti. His head was shaved, and he appeared to be about forty years old. He was allowed to reveal the gift, being trusted to know if someone was ready to receive it. Though it was said that one had only to ask for this gift, the level of sincerity was also weighed.

He sat cross-legged on the stage stairs while we all sat in a half-circle on the floor around him. We were each given a 3x5" index card and a pencil, then instructed to write down our name, address, and phone number. I did so, thinking nothing of it.

Then one by one the participants handed him their card, and after a few questions, he'd indicate whether that person was ready.

I handed him my card, spoke briefly, and he declared: "More listening." He meant that I was not ready and would have to continue attending the discourses.

I had to return. I had to know, no matter what it took, no matter how long. I would continue to attend and wait and wait until I had the answer. After all, the chauvinism that existed in Grotowski's theater had not prevented my experience, so how could this one man's denial stop me? I had no choice but to go forward undaunted.

Years later I would thank this man for refusing me that day. He was right. I was not ready. I was driven by impatience. It is possible I would have taken that gift and discarded it just as quickly without due consideration. We have since become close friends with deep respect and love for one another.

I continued to attend the nightly discourses, listening to one spontaneous speaker after another. It was obvious they were all talking about a tangible experience, though for each it was deeply personal. What stood out was the constant theme: internal peace and the sensation of love it brought with it. But I had a new concern. The idea of joining a group was repugnant to me. Since I left my father's church, I had succeeded in remaining a solitary soul, unencumbered by association with any organization. I was afraid of being lost in the herd. But I continued to listen and wait.

I was still attending O's classes working on my master's piece. I stopped trying to throw myself into light and worked diligently on my project. When O got wind of me attending these meetings, he was furious. He accused me of being poison. I suspect he figured I'd leave the work and possibly inspire the others to leave with me. As if they would! However, O put my continuing to work in the studio, should I take this gift, to a vote among the other students. To my surprise, they voted unanimously to let me stay!

The days became weeks, and the weeks became months. I was a regular at the discourses. The depth of my seriousness became obvious to almost everyone. I began to find out more and more about this Teacher, as my mind put on a royal battle. How afraid was I? And who was this young man, who spoke so beguilingly of something so deep in my heart?

Often, I came home panting with joy, as if I just exited a comprehensive Van Gogh exhibit, bristling with life. I hung back listening very carefully and intently to the message that was being delivered. That there was something within me that could be the source of my experience intrigued me. I was allowed to listen, unencumbered by anyone pushing or prodding me. I attended for myself alone. My journey, as ever, was a solitary one. Fears of being part of a group were set aside. I knew I was not.

The Teacher's precocious nature became obvious early on. As a small boy he would sit on a stage and draw crowds around him by the simple clarity of his message. His father taught him the gift, and when he died the task of continuing to offer this gift was passed on to the young son. Though he continued his education, vacations were spent traveling to speak at events, often in remote regions. He traveled throughout India spreading his message of peace. His fame spread and reached the West when he was just thirteen.

By the time I arrived on the scene, a few years had passed. The Teacher had already married a beautiful, courageous California blonde with a regal quality about her, yet humble.

She had just given birth to their first child. I saw a picture somewhere of them sitting on a sofa together, admiring their lovely little girl. The Teacher was holding the baby so gently in his arms, stroking her little cheeks so lovingly. They were both obviously entranced by the beauty of this new life their love had brought forth. It was a touching scene, though I was not close to them nor did I feel a need to be.

I was there to discover if this was really the key for me. How could it be? I thought. I had searched and pleaded everywhere, now waiting for a key? The debate rang on. Still there was a clear calling from within that kept the need for the question to be answered and the doubt to be resolved.

After several months of waiting, another representative arrived. I was surprised when I came to the hall that night and saw a gorgeous young Indian woman sitting there. She spoke in English, with a softly burning passion, about the beauty of this gift. Then she added, "What difference does it make if I am so beautiful or you are so beautiful? In twenty years neither one of us will be beautiful." I was sure that wasn't true, and one day I would have the chance to tell her.

She mentioned how happy her family was when the Teacher married because it meant that her brother would not feel obliged to choose celibacy over a normal life. Before ending she gave the date and location for our next meeting. It would be in less than two weeks, and I began counting the days. I remember driving home from the hall that night and praying out loud, "Please let this be it, let $X = Y$." I was somewhat startled by the desperation in my voice. Only then did I hear in my own voice how much it meant to me, the hope that after such an exhaustive search, I had finally found the way home.

The meeting took place at a large old turn-of-the-century home on Wilton. I had been there a few times before and arrived in the morning, early for once in my life. About thirty people gathered in the large living room, waiting for the beautiful young woman to arrive. Finally, she arrived in a bit of a flurry. Then everyone settled down, taking a seat on the floor encircling the room against the walls.

She spoke for a while, explaining that if she revealed this gift to anyone before they were truly ready, it would be a problem for her, but it would be an even bigger problem for the receiver. Because, she explained, if one seeks to taste the sweetest fruit, but upon tasting it tosses it away and goes on seeking it, they will never find what they have already passed by.

She began to ask around the circle, one by one, if each was sure they were ready. As I watched and listened to the various responses, I found myself wanting to run for a moment, but I was locked in place, unable to move. I felt as if I was about to jump off a cliff. I knew nothing would ever be the same again. When it was my turn, she just skipped over me and went on to the next person. I think my thirst and my sincerity was obvious.

The gift was revealed unceremoniously in all of its confounding simplicity. We were given plenty of time to practice.

I was exasperated as I climbed into my car, about to be late for work. "How could it be so simple?" I thought to myself. But I had promised to give it chance and practice.

I was working at "Persopolis" a Persian restaurant on Wilshire Boulevard, waiting tables. It was family owned.

The food was delicious, but the music and the belly dancing were even better. I learned to make Moussaka from the owner's wife, who was the chef. She was a kind woman, who looked the other way when I arrived a little late that night.

I could not shake the feeling that I had in fact received something precious that day. My curiosity to experience it led me repeatedly to go into the storage room, where there were no windows, so with the light switched off, it was pitch black. I snuck in and locked the door behind me, just to check and see if the feeling was still there. To my surprise, it was. Not possible, I thought, as I ran back out into the kitchen to grab another order waiting to be delivered. Then as soon as I had a chance, I returned to the darkened storage room to check again. There it was, and each time, more. When I was driving home at 2 am, I was mesmerized. What is this feeling? And how could it have been there all along without me ever knowing it?

In the morning, I kept my promise and practiced it with careful attention. I was able to quiet myself, and in those profoundly still moments I began to notice a peaceful presence opening. I let myself surrender to its subtly increasing beauty, beckoning me to draw nearer. Interesting, I thought, amazing.

When a little over an hour had passed, I stopped and got ready to go to O's class at the studio, late again. As I opened the front door of my apartment and stepped out into the world, I had the distinct impression that something had changed. I wasn't sure what, and it didn't seem to matter. I was different, in some manner I had not expected to be. All the while life was bristling around me. The trees were my brothers. I hopped in my car and started down

Beachwood Drive. I noticed an old lady walking her dog down the sidewalk. Weirdly, I wanted to pull over, get out, pick her and her dog up, toss them into the air, and catch each in either hand. Of course, I did not, but that I, the great cynic, even had that thought like a musical theater moment, was all at once bewildering and amusing.

When I got to class, exercises that had been difficult for me I now performed with relative ease. I was able to do a handstand for the first time in my life. Inversion had always befuddled me.

When we reached the last hour of class, it was time to work on Chi Gung again. I had always dreaded it. But today would be different. Perhaps it was because I had finally understood what concentration really is. Whatever the reason, I found myself able to project light through the palms of my hands.

O was in shock, and for the first time in six years he got up from his desk almost staggering across the room. "She's got it!" Then he told me, "Write, write your name!"

I knew what he meant, and I did it without skipping a beat. I wrote my name in electric blue light in the air! Then O ran to get his friend Stephan Wente from his ballet studio down the hall to come and witness the event.

I was also truly surprised and amazed. However, my interest in the work was not to develop a bag of circus tricks. It was only to complete my master piece and continue tuning up in the process, for whatever could still be gained by studying with Ossetynski. Would it always be as easy as it all seemed today? I wondered, as an afterthought to the elation I felt finishing class that day. Am I different now? What has changed?

I continued to explore the realm within inside myself. "Know thyself" took on a new meaning. Morning and night, I devoted at least an hour to practice the gift. I leapt upon the pillow, where I sat to practice, as if the bed of my lover. Deeper and deeper I went into the spectacular universe within. Filled with peace, I surrendered to the powerful sensation of perfect Love pulsating through me.

More fearless than ever, I was surely invincible I thought, for now I knew the secret of life, the love, and the mercy. My prayers were answered. I was able to enjoy that at will. I admit that at moments it was more love than I could bear, so pure, so forceful—dispelling all sense of the body's boundaries.

I walked through the world as if my feet were not touching the ground. My friends saw something different that they could not describe. I was far less cynical, but it was more than that. I tried to tell them what I was experiencing, but I think it scared them more than encouraged them to check it out. Yet they saw a side of me they'd never seen before: I was happy, and that did cause them to wonder.

Eventually, I went out to see my parents. Their reaction to my arrival at the front door was different. Normally, at least my father would rush to embrace me. Mother would linger a little behind before greeting me with her feathery hugs. This time they both stepped back, as if I was taking more space than usual.

As our afternoon together ensued, I tried to tell them about the wonderful new experience I was having and how I came by it. At first, Dad was not at all impressed. "How could such a young man be able to reveal that?"

Seriously? I thought. Now I was also insulted. I raised my finger to him and said, "You raised me. You taught me theology. Do you think I don't know the difference between the Truth and a trick?"

He fell silent.

Sometime later I would invite them both out to dinner and to attend a discourse. The man who spoke that night had been a Professor of Physics at UCLA. His credentials impressed my father's scientific mind, and he listened attentively, elbows on knees and face in hands. Afterwards, I invited them up to my little place for a dessert of sweet apples sautéed with cinnamon and a dollop of sour cream before their long way home. We parted peacefully that day and never fought about this again.

Later I thought to myself, even if they had loved me more than each other, to the exclusion of all and everyone else, it would not have been enough! The love I had always sought was the one I have within me, the perfect love. The love that had always been with me, and only now, had I found it.

To Be Continued

Acknowledgements

I am Grateful...

To John F. Quinlan and Jeanette Blanche (Witkowski) Quinlan, my parents, for their love and individual roles in shaping my character.

To Ora Cummings, my agent, for her enthusiasm, kindness, excellent editing and genuine friendship.

To Ian Hooper, my publisher, for reading it, loving it, and giving it a chance.

To Sherry Weinstein for her watchful eye, considered comments and loving inspiration.

To Mark William Spradley, for his steadfast honesty and unwavering loyalty.

To Steven Whitney, for his professional advice and his extraordinary generosity.

To Kathleen Mary Quinlan, for her constant love and guidance.

To Raphael "Ella" Quinlan, my daughter, for all she has taught me about compassion, tolerance and Love.

And finally, to Timothy Gallwey, my loving husband, for all that he is to me, my lover, my protector, and of course, my coach!

About the Author

Barbara Ann Quinlan was born in upstate New York and later raised in Southern California. For six years, she studied a radical form of eastern European theater; first with Leonidas Dudarew-Ossentynski at his studio in Hollywood and then at the Theater Laboratory of Jerzy Grotowski, in Wrocław, Poland.

Her studies included No and Kabuki Theater, ancient Chinese resonator techniques for the voice, Thai Chi and Chi gung, among countless other exercises aimed at breaking down one's resistances in order to develop the actor as a superhuman; capable of performing far beyond the normal human range.

Barbara wrote her first poem at five and has kept numerous journals. She studied French in Paris, Spanish in school and Hebrew in Israel. Throughout the years, she has used her knowledge of Chi gung to perform energetic healing.

After spending ten years traveling as the executive assistant to a well-known author who gives seminars around the world, Barbara now dedicates herself to the joys of life itself, her family, her friends and her writing.

Made in the USA
Middletown, DE
25 June 2022